Contents:

GREAT EXPECTATIONS CHAPTER SUMMARIES

Italicised words can be found in the lists of **Named Characters** or **Places**

Part 1

Chapters 1-19

Part one of Great Expectations takes the narrator, *Pip*, from being a seven-year-old orphan in the house of his twenty-seven-year-old sister and her blacksmith husband, *Joe Gargery*, living in a small village on the north Kent[1] marshes, to being an eighteen-year-old[2] young gentleman in training on his way to London with Great Expectations.

Chapter 1

Seven-year-old *Pip* is visiting the graveyard where his parents and four older brother are buried. It is a cold and foggy day (actually Christmas Eve) in the north Kent marshes. A man rise up from among the graves - he is dressed in grey, filthy, bloody and cold, and has shackles on his legs. He makes the terrified *Pip* tell him where he lives, and on discovering that it at the local blacksmith's, makes him promise to bring him 'wittles' (victuals) and a metal file. On pain of death (at the hands of an unseen accomplice who will follow him) he is to tell nobody and to bring the goods to the old *battery* the next morning.

Chapter 2

When *Pip* gets home he is warned by his kindly foster father *Joe Gargery*, the village blacksmith, that his waspish sister, who is *Joe*'s wife (*Mrs. Joe*), is out looking for him and 'on the rampage.' She has taken *Tickler* with her. We are introduced to her on her return. *Pip* hides his bread and butter tea down his trouser leg for the man in the graveyard, is accused of bolting it down and made to drink tar-water, a foul tasting 'cure'. They hear canon-fire from across the marshes, signifying the escape of a prisoner from the *hulks*. *Joe* confirms that this is the second escape in as many days. *Pip* sleeps badly, and at first light, raids the pantry, taking odd bits of food, some brandy and a pork pie. He then takes one of *Joe*'s files from the *forge*.

Chapter 3

Pip makes his way to the *battery* through mist and rain. He see a convict sitting with his back to him and approaches, but it is not his convict. The man runs off. *Pip* finds his convict at the *battery* as arranged and hands over the food and file. They talk while the convict is eating greedily and filing away at his shackles. *Pip* is polite and deferential, and the convict becomes more trusting. *Pip* mentions having seen the accomplice and the convict (who had actually made this up to scare *Pip* into doing as he demanded) and wants to know more. When *Pip* mentions a bruise on his face, the convict asks which way he ran. *Pip* leaves for home with the convict still filing away at the shackles.

Chapter 4

On *Pip*'s return home, the missing food has not been noticed with *Mrs Joe* bad-temperedly preparing Christmas dinner. *Pip* and *Joe* are shooed off to church for the morning carol service, *Pip* feeling guilty about taking the food and fearful of discovery. *Mrs Joe* has invited *Woplse*, *Mr and Mrs Hubble* and *Pumblechook* for dinner. They all seem to enjoy prodding *Pip* with 'moral goads', and giving him scanty food, but *Joe* keeps feeding him gravy. *Pumblechook* is given brandy, but it turns out that *Pip* accidentally used tar water to top it up when taking some for the convict. *Pip* runs to the door in panic, and into some soldiers.

Chapter 5

The soldiers are looking for the blacksmith to repair some handcuffs. *Joe* says it will take two hours, as the forge fire needs to be lit. That will just give them time to set out looking for the convict before dark.[3] *Pumblechook* shares round the gift of sherry and port he had brought for *Mrs Joe* while *Joe* mends the cuffs, then the soldiers set off in pursuit of the convicts, accompanied by *Joe, Pip* and *Woplse*. Out past the church they hear a shout, and find the two convicts fighting in a ditch. *Pip*'s convict says he called out because he'd caught the other, the other that *Pip*'s convict was trying to kill him. *Pip* signals to his convict that he didn't give him away, and the convicts are taken off with *Joe, Woplse* and *Pip* following. In a military hut, *Pip*'s convict claims that he broke into the blacksmith's and stole food. The convicts are rowed back to the *hulks*.

Chapter 6

Pip wonders whether he should tell *Joe* about the file, but fears losing the trust and affection of his only friend. *Joe* carries the sleepy *Pip* home. Upon arrival, he tells *Mrs Joe* and the guests about the convict's confession, and there is much fanciful speculation as to how the robbery was achieved.

Chapter 7

A year has passed. Previously, *Pip* had had no formal education[4], but now he attends a village evening school of no educational merit run by *Mr Woplse's* Great Aunt in a rented cottage in whose upper room *Woplse* indulges his love of amateur dramatics during lesson times. A fellow student is the school-mistress's grand-daughter, *Biddy*, a neglected and unkempt orphan. We learn that *Joe's* father, also a blacksmith, was a drunkard who beat his wife and child, and would not let *Joe* be educated. He is illiterate, but does not admit to it, and *Pip* decides to pass on what little education he gets to *Joe*. We also learn that *Joe's* parents both dies when he was a young man, and that he was lonely when he met *Pip*'s sister - 'a fine figure of a woman'. Although her (and *Pip*'s) parents had already died and she was already bringing *Pip* up 'by hand' he was very small and weak, so presumably she was not doing a very good job of it. *Joe* believes she won't approve of his being educated. It's market day, and *Mrs Joe* is out at the market helping the unmarried *Pumblechook*. They arrive back in high spirits bursting with the news that the 'immensely rich and grim' *Miss Havisham*, a resident of the nearby town, asked *Pumblechook*, a tenant of hers, if he knew of a young boy to go to her house to play, and he suggested *Pip*. *Pumblechook* and *Mrs Joe* are clearly excited about the possible benefits that might come to them - so *Pip* is washed and brushed up and leaves with *Pumblechook* to be presented to *Miss Havisham* the next day.

Chapter 8

While tucking into a rather better breakfast than he gives *Pip, Pumblechook* tests *Pip* constantly of arithmetic. At ten o'clock they walk to *Satis House* and ring the bell. A 'young lady' of about *Pip*'s age comes to the door and takes *Pip* in. The house is dark inside and the only light is from the young lady's candle. She takes *Pip* to a door, tells him to knock, and leaves. He enters a ladies dressing room, lit only by candles (the heavy curtains being closed, as everywhere in the house). A 'shrunken and withered' woman[5] - *Miss Havisham* - sits there in as faded bridal dress. All the clocks are stopped at twenty to nine[6]. *Pip* introduces himself and she informs him that her heart is broken, then instructs him to play. He understandably says he can't and she calls the young lady - *Estella* - to come and play cards with him. *Miss Havisham* shows a blatant preference for *Estella* and tells *Pip* that that *Estella* can break his heart. He is made to feel clumsy and stupid and loses twice at 'beggar my neighbour'. *Miss Havisham* asks *Pip* to whisper to her what he thinks of *Estella*, and he says she is very proud, pretty and insulting and that he would like to go home. She makes an appointment for him to return in six days' time. *Estella* leads him out and he is given bread meat and beer[7]. He explores the disused brewery attached to the house and the grounds annoyed at his sensitivity and timidity and deeply stung by being called coarse and common. He imagines he sees *Estella*, his chief taunter, everywhere. When she comes to let him out she rubs further salt into his wounds by asking why he doesn't cry (he did when left to explore). He walks the four miles back to the *forge* feeling discontented with who he is.

Chapter 9

On *Pip*'s return home *Mrs Joe* is curious about *Pip*'s experiences. He doesn't want to talk about it because his feelings are still all over the place. *Mrs Joe* is insistent, however, so he invents a preposterous story. When *Joe* comes in for tea, *Mrs Joe* repeats this to him and he is amazed. While *Mrs Joe* and *Pumblechook* further discuss what benefits might come from the association, *Pip* goes out to *Joe*, who has returned to the *forge*. *Pip* is deeply unhappy that *Joe* should have believed his story and admits that he was lying, and how he felt bad about being common. *Joe* tells him that lying isn't the way to get out of being common, and he mustn't lie any more. *Pip*, however, is beginning to worry how common *Joe* and *Mrs Joe* were also. He, as narrator, sees that day as the first link in the chain of the rest of his life.

Chapter 10

Pip decides to become educated to be less common. He asks *Biddy,* who is an exceptionally quick learner, to teach him. She indeed takes over teaching the whole class while her incompetent grandmother sleeps during lessons. After the lesson, *Pip* is under instructions from *Mrs Joe* to stop at the *Three Jolly Bargemen* to collect *Joe*, who, it being a Saturday, has gone there to relax. *Joe* and *Woplse* are sitting with a stranger - a 'secret looking man'. The stranger turns the conversation to runaway convicts and questions *Joe* about who *Pip* is then, invisibly to *Joe* and *Woplse*, but pointedly to *Pip*, he stirs his rum with the file *Pip* had taken for the convict. When *Joe* gets up to leave, the stranger hands *Pip* a 'bright shilling'[8] wrapped up in crumpled paper. Back home it is discovered that the crumpled paper was in fact two one pound notes[9]. Sure it's a mistake, *Joe* rushes back to the pub to return the money, but the stranger is gone. *Mrs Joe* puts it in a safe place to return to him should he ever come back.

Chapter 11

On his second visit to *Miss Havisham*, *Pip* is led by *Estella* to a different room where *Miss Havisham*'s relatives *Sarah Pocket, Georgiana* and *Camilla*, and her husband *Raymond* are gathered - 'all toadies and humbugs' even to the young *Pip*'s eyes. They are disparagingly discussing another cousin, *Matthew Pocket*. On the ring of a distant bell *Estella* leads *Pip* away. In their discussion it is clear that *Miss Havisham* has told *Estella* the things *Pip* thought he was telling her about *Estella* in confidence. On the stairs they pass a man (who later to be shown to be the attorney *Jaggers*) who questions *Pip* briefly. *Pip* is sent to a large room opposite *Miss Havisham*'s dressing room - again heavily curtained and candle-lit with a long table with a centrepiece covered in mould and cobwebs - and spiders. *Miss Havisham* says she will be laid out on the table when she dies, and identifies the centrepiece as her wedding cake. She asks *Pip* to walk her round and round the room. *Estella* enters with the cousins, who further demonstrate themselves to be 'toadies and humbugs', before being dismissed, and led away by *Estella*. *Miss Havisham* says that it is her birthday, which is why the cousins are there, but they are not allowed to mention it. It was on her birthday, long before *Pip* was born, that she was to have been married. It is clear that time, like the clocks, has been stopped in the house since then - nothing changed and no daylight let in. She command *Pip* to play at cards again with *Estella*, and keeps drawing *Pip*'s attention to *Estella*'s beauty. The date of the next visit is set, and *Pip* is again led away, fed, and allowed to wander. A *'pale young gentleman'* of about his age comes out of a separate house in the grounds of the manor house (*Satis House*) and challenges *Pip* to a boxing match. The young gentleman appears very expert, but in reality has no defence, and *Pip* repeatedly knocks him down - he finally throws in the sponge after hitting his head on a wall as he goes down. *Pip* doesn't know that *Estella* has been watching, but she looks very elated when seeing him out and tells him he may kiss her, which he does, on the cheek. It is dark by the time he gets home.

Chapter 12

Being of humble birth and sensitive and timid by nature, *Pip* is worried that he might be punished for fighting a gentleman and fears returning to *Satis House*, but the pale young gentleman has left and no mention is made of him. There is a wheelchair which *Pip* is to push *Miss Havisham* around in, and he is to come each second day at noon for the next eight to ten months for that purpose. She asks him a lot of questions about himself, but never offers money or help with education. She does, on the other hand, keep taunting him with how pretty *Estella* is growing. *Biddy* becomes *Pip*'s confidante - indeed the only person he felt able to discuss his experiences with. *Pumblechook* continued to combine talking disparagingly about *Pip*'s prospects with ridiculous speculations about what *Miss Havisham* would do for *Pip*. One day *Miss Havisham* comments on how tall *Pip* is growing, and on the next visit she instructs him to bring *Joe* with him on his next visit, along with his indentures[10]. On hearing this, *Mrs Joe* goes on the rampage - clearly hoping for something more from *Miss Havisham* - and into a cleaning frenzy.

Chapter 13

Pip is uncomfortable about *Joe*'s choice of his Sunday best clothes for the trip to *Miss Havisham* - partly on *Joe*'s behalf that he should make himself uncomfortable, but also his unquestioning affection for *Joe* is beginning to give way to a more critical attitude. This is normal for his age, but also heightened by his contact with *Miss Havisham* and *Estella*. They walk to the town, accompanied by *Mrs Joe*, who waits with *Pumblechook*. When *Miss Havisham* quizzes *Joe* about *Pip*, he addresses his answers to *Pip*, which *Pip* finds embarrassing - all the more so because *Estella*'s expression seems to imply that she finds *Joe* comical. When *Joe* assures *Miss Havisham* that it is *Pip*'s heart's wish to be apprenticed to him, he is keenly aware that this is no longer the case. But *Miss Havisham* accepts the truth of it and pays *Joe* an indenture premium of twenty-five Guineas[11]. *Miss Havisham* bids *Pip* goodbye: 'Gargery is your master now.' There is no goodbye from *Estella*. Back at *Pumblechook*'s, *Joe* teases *Mrs Joe* and *Pumblechook* about the size of the premium, but both think the amount very generous. *Pumblechook* insists that *Pip* be legally 'bound out of hand' to the apprenticeship[12] and they all go to the courthouse to get the paperwork done. *Mrs Joe* insists on a celebratory dinner at the *Blue Boar*, and *Pumblechook* takes his cart to fetch *Woplse* and the *Hubble*'s to join them. Back home and in bed, a wretched *Pip* is certain that this is no longer what he wants.

Chapter 14

Pip is ashamed of his home and miserable about it. He feels that his home is as coarse and common as *Estella* accused him of being. The apprenticeship feels like a life sentence to his. He is made wretched be the feeling of the betrayal of *Joe* it would be not go through with it but haunted by the idea of *Estella* seeing him at work and despising him for it: he keeps imagining he sees her doing just that.

Chapter 15

Time has passed. *Pip* has finished at the village school, but continues to be taught by *Biddy*. Perhaps out of a mixture of genuine concern for *Joe* and his own embarrassment at *Joe's* ignorance, *Pip* decides to teach *Joe* what he is learning from *Biddy*. *Mrs Joe* being against *Joe's* education, lessons take place at the *old battery*. *Joe* seems contented and attentive, but never seems to learn anything or remember anything. *Miss Havisham* and *Estella* still haunt *Pip*, and one day he asks *Joe* if he thinks he should pay *Miss Havisham* a visit. *Joe* advises against it, lest *Miss Havisham* should think *Pip* was looking for more money. *Pip* argues that he never said thank-you. He asks *Joe* for a half day off so he can pay a visit, almost letting slip that it's actually *Estella* he wants to see. *Joe* relents, but tells *Pip* he must not try again if he is not welcome there. We are introduced to Dolge *Orlick*, a journeyman[13] who has worked for *Joe* on and off since *Pip* was small. He is about twenty-five (so he presumably learned the trade from *Joe*, since he would have been still in his mid-teens when *Pip* came to live with *Joe*) and described as morose and of 'slouching demeanour'. He lodges with a sluice-keeper out on the marshes. *Pip* believes that he is jealous of his having been apprenticed, and *Orlick* indeed asks why he can't also have a half-holiday. *Joe* agrees, as *Orlick* is a good worker, but *Mrs Joe* objects. He insults her under his breath, but is heard. *Joe* defends his wife, but *Mrs Joe* insists that he fight *Orlick*. *Joe* is physically very strong, and wins the fight easily. *Pip* goes to get changed and, on his return, finds *Joe* and *Orlick* peacefully sweeping up. When *Pip* arrives at *Satis House*, it is *Sarah Pocket* who comes to unlock the gate. He talks briefly to *Miss Havisham* who says he may visit now and then, and should come next on his birthday. She tells him that *Estella* is abroad, and prettier than ever, malignantly adding 'do you feel that you have lost her?' He is then dismissed, more discontented than ever. Walking back through the town he meets *Woplse* coming out of a bookshop and invited to come with him to *Pumblechook's* where he is to read from a murder story. *Woplse* and *Pip* finally leave for home at 9.30 in the evening, being joined by *Orlick* along the way. They hear the canons firing out on the *hulks*, meaning another prisoner had escaped. They reach the *Three Jolly Bargemen* at eleven o'clock and are surprised to see it in commotion. *Joe's* house had been entered, they are told, and somebody attacked. When they reach the house it is full of people. *Mrs Joe* has suffered a severe blow from behind. It is supposed that she was attacked by an escaped convict.

Chapter 16

Pip, his head full of the murder story read by *Woplse*, is immediately, if a little fancifully, more concerned about suspicion falling on him than he is about his sister's welfare. The police are there and narrowing down the time of the attack and who was where at that time. It appears that *Mrs Joe* was struck by a convict's leg iron, but *Joe*, on inspecting it, says it was filed some time ago. Nothing has been taken, so the motive does not appear to have been theft. *Pip* wonders to himself whether either *Orlick*, who would have had a grievance, or the stranger who had given him a shilling might have attacked *Mrs Joe*. Either of them might have found the leg iron (*Orlick* living on the marsh and the stranger being in possession of the file). But *Orlick* has an alibi, and the stranger has no motive. *Pip* continues to agonise about whether he should have told *Joe* about 'his' convict, but fears *Joe* might now suspect him of lying (after his stories about *Satis House*), in addition to his earlier concerns. The police are around for a week or so, but unable to solve the crime. As narrator, *Pip* observes that they 'persisted in trying to fit the circumstances to the [wrong] ideas, instead of trying to extract ideas from the circumstances.' A valuable caution. *Mrs Joe* is bed-ridden for a long time after the assault, her vision, speech and memory permanently impaired, but her temper improved, *Pip* the narrator observes. Not long after this, *Biddy*'s grandmother dies, and *Joe* takes her into his care in return for the housekeeping duties *Mrs Joe* can no longer perform, as well as to look after *Mrs Joe*. *Mrs Joe*, as she recovered a little, had frequently drawn a sort of T on a slate[14]. *Pip* had asked her if it were a hammer, which seemed to be almost but not quite right. When *Biddy* joins the household, *Mrs Joe* draws the T-shape again, and *Biddy* immediately guesses that she means *Orlick* with his hammer. When Orlick is brought, *Pip* expects her to confirm his guilt, but instead she seems anxious in his presence.

Chapter 17

Pip has settled into a routine as apprentice. On his birthday, he makes the agreed visit to *Miss Havisham*. It follows the established course - *Estella* is still away, and, during the brief visit, *Miss Havisham* provokes *Pip* by talking about her and how beautiful she is. She establishes an ongoing routine of giving *Pip* a guinea on his birthday, and stirs up his dissatisfaction with his life. *Pip* notices that *Biddy* is becoming a woman. She is still and kind and sweet tempered, but now takes more care of her appearance. And she is still able to absorb knowledge seemingly effortlessly: *Pip* spends his birthday guinea of his own education, but she always seems always one step ahead of him. Even in blacksmithing, she seems to know what he knows. *Pip* is so fixated on *Estella* that it never occurs to him the *Biddy* might be doing this to get closer to him. They arrange to take walk together next Sunday. It is summertime and they walk out onto the marshes. *Pip* confides to *Biddy* that he wants to be a gentleman. *Biddy* is not sure that would make him happy, and *Pip* thoughtlessly talks about how he might once have been happy to be married to *Biddy*, and how he was made to feel coarse and common by a beautiful young lady and he wants to be a gentleman on her account. *Biddy* asks if this is to spite her or to gain her, and that he's be better off ignoring her as she didn't sound worth gaining. *Pip* admits to the truth of this but admits to admiring her 'dreadfully'. But what did it matter, as he would never be a gentleman. As they walk on, he wonders to himself why he doesn't prefer *Biddy* who is not insulting or capricious and doesn't make him feel miserable over *Estella* who is and does. On the way back they come across *Orlick*, slouching around, as ever. *Biddy* admits to not liking *Orlick* because she fears that he likes her - he 'dances at her'. *Pip* considers getting him fired, but is worried on account of *Mrs Joe*'s new-found respect for him. Life goes on in a similar vein, *Pip* slowly growing contented then his contentment being shattered by a memory of his times at *Satis House*. He still wonders if, after all, *Miss Havisham* wasn't going to make his fortune when his apprenticeship was complete.

Chapter 18

Pip is in the fourth year of his apprenticeship and spending a Saturday evening in the *Three Jolly Bargemen* as part of a group including *Joe* and *Woplse*. *Woplse* is reading aloud from a newspaper concerning a notorious murder, acting out the characters in the story and drawing the assembled company to the conclusion that the accused must be guilty. A stranger starts to contest *Wopsle*'s conclusions using a barrister's bullying techniques. *Pip* recognises as the attorney *Jaggers*, who he saw on his second visit to *Miss Havisham*. Having dealt with *Wopsle*, *Jaggers* says he wants to see the blacksmith, and then his apprentice, *Pip*. The three of them leave for *Joe*'s house where *Jaggers* introduces himself as the 'confidential agent of another'. He asks if *Joe* would want compensation for releasing *Pip* from his apprenticeship, and *Joe* says that of course he wouldn't want money if that's what *Pip* wanted. *Jaggers* announces that *Pip* has 'great expectations' - that he will come into a handsome property. In the meanwhile he is to be taken away and brought up as a gentleman. There are two conditions: first that he will always be called *Pip* (not his actual name of *Philip Pirrip*), and second that he should never try to find out who his benefactor is. *Pip* naturally assumes, however that it is *Miss Havisham*, as *Pumblechook* and *Mrs Joe* have always hoped. He readily agrees and *Jaggers* tells him that he, *Jaggers*, was appointed guardian money for *Mr Pip*'s education and maintenance was already in his hands. With a lawyer's carefulness he mentions the name of (not recommends) *Matthew Pocket* as a tutor - a name *Pip* recognises from the discussion between *Miss Havisham*'s relatives. Glancing at *Joe* for confirmation that it's Ok, *Pip* says he will go to *London* directly. *Jaggers* hands him twenty guineas for clothes. *Joe* is offered a gift of money also, but says that *Pip* is free to go with his blessing but no money could compensate. *Jaggers* tells *Pip* to come to his *London* address in one week's time. *Pip* is once more torn apart by his loathing of his circumstances and the goodness of *Joe* and *Biddy*.

Chapter 19

Pip's ridiculous fears about what could go wrong indicate just how much he wants what's on offer. *Joe* burns the indentures, showing he has no claim on *Pip*. *Pip* walks out on the marshes and feels sorry for those who must live out their lives there. He thinks about how the convict he helped is probably either deported or dead. He walks out to the *old battery* and falls asleep wondering if *Miss Havisham* is doing this to make him good enough for *Estella*. He wakes up to find *Joe* next to him and tells him how he has always wanted to be a gentleman, but promises he'll never forget *Joe*. Back at the forge he asks *Diddy* to help *Joe* with his lessons, suggesting that when he comes into his money he can then get *Joe* a better position. *Biddy* asks *Pip* if he has never considered that *Joe* might rather be too proud to let anybody take him from where he is known and respected. *Pip* thinks that she is just envious of him. He walks off feeling bad again. The next day he visits *Mr Trabb* the tailor, whose attitude to him changes immediately from casual to attentive when he hears he has come into property. *Pip* orders a fashionable suit of clothes to be delivered to *Mr Pumblechook*'s on the following Thursday evening, the day being Monday. He visits other shops for shoes and hats and books a place on the London coach for 7am the following Saturday, noticing how the traders immediately give their full attention on hearing he has come into property. He then visits *Pumblechook* who feeds and wines him and proceeds to re-write the history of their relationship with himself as the benevolent uncle who always believed in *Pip* - before suggesting that *Pip* might invest in his business. *Pip* walks a little way down the road and sleeps off the wine under a hedge. The following Friday he collects the clothes while *Pumblechook* is out and wears them to go to *Satis House*. Certain that *Miss Havisham* is his benefactor but aware that he may not make it known to her that he knows, he is sure that he must at least tell her that he is leaving for London the next day, somehow implying his gratitude. She tells him she has heard of his good fortune from *Jaggers* and tells him to be good, deserve it and follow *Jaggers'* instructions. While serving to confirm *Pip*'s belief to him - and she seems quite aware of what she is doing, it serves the dual purpose of goading *Sarah Pocket* with the thought that she is bestowing a large portion of her fortune on *Pip*, leaving less for her. *Pip* drops to his knee and kisses her hand as he takes his leave. Back at *Pumblechook*'s he changes back into his old clothes and heads back to the village, bundled up new suit with him. He dresses up to show *Joe* and *Biddy* then goes to bed, having to be up at five o'clock the next day to catch the coach. He is still conflicted between love of them and embarrassment to be associated with them, and is glad to walk off alone, though he comes to his senses temporarily on the way, leaning against the signpost and crying, then several times being on the point of getting off the coach and returning home.

Italicised words can be found in the lists of **Named Characters** or **Places**

Part 2

Chapters 20-39

Part two takes the narrator, *Pip*, from his arrival in London as an eighteen-year old ex-apprentice blacksmith from a small village in the north Kent marshes who has just been told of his great expectations to a twenty-three-year-old gentleman living in London who has just met the person responsible for his change of fortunes - and is horrified at the discovery of who it is.

Chapter 20

The coach journey from *Pip*'s town to *London* takes 5 hours, so he arrives around mid-day. He finds *London* ugly and dirty. Taking a (horse-drawn) cab to *Jaggers*' office in *Little Britain*, he finds even the driver fearful of *Jaggers*' reputation. *Jaggers* is out, however, on *Pip*'s arrival, and a clerk asks him to wait in *Jaggers*' office - a surprisingly small and dreary place. *Pip* finds the summer stuffiness unbearable, and goes for a walk while he waits, passing *Smithfield* meat market, *St Paul's* cathedral and *Newgate* prison, where he is shown the gallows by a drunken official. On a second expedition, having checked in at the office again, encounters *Jaggers* on his way there, dealing briskly with clients crowding round him and usually ending the encounter with the question 'have you paid *Wemmick*?' Back in his office, *Jaggers* informs *Pip* that he is to stay at *Barnard's Inn* with *Matthew Pocket*'s son, *Herbert*, over the weekend before going to *Matthew* (to start his education) on Monday. He is also told how much his generous living allowance will be and told the arrangements for making purchases, so that *Jaggers*, as his guardian, can keep an eye n his expenditure. In his typical lawyer's style he makes sure that *Pip* realises that if, however, he does overspend then *Jaggers* cannot be held responsible. *Wemmick*, who turns out to be the clerk *Pip* spoke to on his arrival, will escort *Pip* to *Barnard's Inn*.

Chapter 21

The walk from *Little Britain* to *Barnard's Inn* allows *Pip* to observe and begin to get to know *Wemmick*: in particular, he notices a somewhat dry and stiff demeanour and a lot of old watch chains and rings and the like adorning him. *Pip*, used as he was to coaching inns, had assumed *Barnard's Inn* to be a hotel, but it proves to be a rather dingy selection of shabby apartments. *Wemmick* leads him upstairs to the top floor chambers where *Herbert Pocket* lives then leaves, telling *Pip* that as he's in charge of the money, they will probably meet often. *Herbert* is out - a note saying he'd be back soon - and as *Pip* waits for him he reflects that *London* is decidedly overrated. When *Herbert* arrives, *Pip* sees he is a gentleman of about his own age and social standing. He had been to *Covent Garden* market to buy fruit for *Pip*'s arrival. *Jaggers* has instructed the local coffee shop to supply the food while *Pip* stays at *Pip*'s expense. *Herbert* explains that the shabby place is all he can afford, as he has to make his own way life. He suddenly recognises *Pip* as the 'prowling boy' from *Satis House*: *Pip* has already recognised the 'pale young gentleman' (Ch.11)

Chapter 22

Despite their unfortunate first encounter, *Pip* and *Herbert* now make instant friends - although *Pip* notices that *Herbert* still has a tendency to confuse his intention with his execution of an idea, as in their boxing encounter. *Herbert* explains that *Miss Havisham* had sent for him (his father, *Matthew*, being a relative of hers) to see if he was suitable for *Estella*. It was a trial visit, and he believes that he might have been provided for and engaged to if *Estella* had liked him, but she didn't. *Pip*'s ears prick up at this point: he already believes that *Miss Havisham* is responsible for his money, and *Herbert*'s comments seem to confirm that being promised to *Estella* is part of the deal. *Herbert*, however is sure that he had a lucky escape: *Estella*, who *Miss Havisham* adopted, is hard and capricious and brought up by *Miss Havisham* to wreak revenge on all the male sex. *Pip* wonders why this should be, and *Herbert* promises to tell him over lunch, but first he wants to know how *Pip* came to be at *Satis House*, and if *Jaggers* is his guardian, and if he knows that *Jaggers* is *Miss Havisham*'s solicitor and business manager. While to *Pip* this is further confirmation that *Miss Havisham* is responsible for his great expectations, he is aware that he must not openly speculate about it. He does however tell that to *Herbert*, along with answering his questions. More anxious than ever to get on with becoming a gentleman, *Pip* asks *Herbert* to be his guide on matters of etiquette, which *Herbert* does in a good-natured but humorous way throughout their lunch. He doesn't, however, like the name Phillip (*Pip*'s real name) and chooses to call him *Handel* - a rather contrived reference to 'The Harmonious Blacksmith' by the composer George Frideric Handel, alluding to *Pip*'s past occupation and to the harmony of their future friendship - rather than '*Pip*'. Over a rather chaotic dinner, *Herbert* tells *Pip Miss Havisham*'s story. *Miss Havisham* was a spoilt child - her mother died when she was a baby, but her father was a wealthy country gentleman and brewer. He later remarried secretly - *Herbert* believes it was his cook - and had a son who, unlike his mother, was acknowledged. The son, however, turned out bad and was disinherited, although the father relented before he died and gave him a generous living allowance, though the bulk of the fortune went to *Miss Havisham*. 25 years ago[15] her brother teamed up with a suave conman[16] who wooed her and she fell passionately in love with. He conned her out of a lot of money before jilting her on her wedding day. *Herbert*'s father *Matthew* was the only person to warn *Miss Havisham* about this man and was sent packing for his pains. They have not met since. *Miss Havisham* received the letter telling her the wedding was off at twenty to nine on the morning of her wedding day - the time at which the clocks all now stand, suggesting her life stopped at that moment. The curtains were closed, and she has not seen daylight since that moment. *Herbert* has no idea what ultimately became of the half-brother or the conman - even if they are still alive. *Estella*, he confirms, was adopted at a young age[17] but that's all he knows. *Herbert* describes himself as a capitalist, and insurer of ships, but *Pip* quickly sees this as another example of mistaking the wish for the reality. They go to the theatre that evening and to church together the next day, which is Sunday. *Pip* accompanies *Herbert* to a grimy counting-house[18] where he habitually looks for money-making opportunities, then both leave for *Hammersmith*, where *Matthew Pocket* lives, at noon. They arrive mid-afternoon to find the scatty *Mrs Pocket*, two nursemaids and seven young *Pocket* children in the garden. *Mr Pocket*, grey-haired and with a permanently perplexed expression, come out to greet *Pip*.

Chapter 23

Mrs Pocket is the only daughter of a somewhat delusional father who imagined himself of a higher social status than he was, and brought her up to be ornamental not practical. *Matthew Pocket*, in his youth, had the same over-optimistic view of his prospects that his son has inherited. There are two other young gentlemen lodging with them and receiving an education - *Startop* and *Drummle*, the next but one heir to a baronetcy[19] . We are shown various aspects of the *Pockets*' domestic life. This is to be *Pip*'s place of residence.

Chapter 24

Pip is to spend the next two or three days at *Matthew Pocket*'s house receiving advice and suggestions about places to visit. He builds a good relationship with *Matthew*, but decides to keep his place at *Barnard's Inn*, buying the furniture that was hired for him. *Pip* talks to *Wemmick* about *Jaggers'* not very encouraging attitude, and is assured he is only being professional. He also learns more from *Wemmick* about *Jaggers'* work and about 'portable property' - the small personal possessions (rings and the like) *Wemmick* gets from condemned prisoners or grateful clients found innocent. *Wemmick* invites *Pip* to visit him and home, and asks if he's dined with *Jaggers* yet: - certain that the invitation will come, *Wemmick* tells *Pip* to take a good look at *Jaggers'* housekeeper when there, as 'a wild beast tamed[20]'. *Wemmick* takes *Pip* along to the court to watch *Jaggers* at work, and it's clear that everybody, even the magistrate, is nervously in awe of him.

Chapter 25

Every now and then, Dickens reminds us that the story is being written by *Pip* at a later time - probably when he is in his mid-thirties when the story ends. The extent of his dislike for *Bentley Drummle* even at this stage is clearly written with the perspective of later events - but the description is very unfavourable. *Startop* he describes as being delicate and spoilt by his mother, but a much preferred companion. *Pip* pays frequent visits to *Barnard's Inn*. A month or two later, *Matthew Pocket* has a visit from his sister *Camilla,* with her husband *Raymond* and cousin *Georgiana* (all of whom *Pip* remembers from *Satis House*)- and they all make their dislike of *Pip* clear - they also assume that his fortune is from *Miss Havisham*, and is thus coming out the inheritance they are hoping for. *Pip* is beginning to slip into over-spending, as *Jaggers* predicted, but has not visited *Little Britain* for several weeks when he decides to take *Wemmick* up on his invitation and visit him at home. He meets him at the office at six o'clock, and they decide to walk to *Walworth* together. *Wemmick* asks again if *Pip* has dined with *Jaggers* and tells him the invitation will come soon, and will be extended to his 'pals' also - unfortunately including *Drummle* along with *Herbert* and *Startop*. *Wemmick*'s house is a tine wooden cottage made, by *Wemmick*'s own carpentry, to look like a *Castle*[21]. The house has a moat - not much more than a ditch in reality - and *Wemmick* keeps livestock and grows vegetables as 'provisions against siege'. He shares the house with his deaf father, the *Aged Parent*. *Wemmick* explains that his home world and office world are completely separate and must remain so. Walking back to the office together the next morning *Pip* watches as *Wemmick*'s whimsical home self slowly morphs into his stiff, dry work self.

Chapter 26

As predicted, the dinner invitation from *Jaggers* comes and he takes his guests from his office to his *Soho* home - a fine building but in want of redecoration. *Jaggers* takes an irrational liking to *Drummle*, though calling him the *Spider* (correctly diagnosing his character as one prepared to sit and wait for his moment like a spider in a web) and describing him in unflattering terms. He ignores *Startop*. As suggested by *Wemmick*, *Pip* observes the housekeeper. She is about forty years old, with a lot of hair and a disturbed-looking face. She is very watchful and cautions around *Jaggers*. Unlike *Wemmick*, *Jaggers* home persona is exactly the same as his work persona (despite his almost obsessive washing of his hands before leaving work) - and he proceeds to draw out the worst in his guests. After inciting the slightly drunk young men to show their muscles, *Jaggers* rather alarmingly seizes his housekeeper, *Molly*, by the hand and insists that she show her wrists, one of which is disfigured. *Jaggers* says she has more power in her wrists than most men, then lets her go. After more to drink all round *Pip* gets into an argument with *Drummle*, who shows his contempt for his companions. As a fight nearly beaks out, *Jaggers*, who has to some extent engineered the situation, points out that the agreed finishing time of 9.30 has arrived and the party breaks up. *Pip* goes back to apologise to *Jaggers* who repeats that he likes the *Spider* as 'one of the true sort' - but advises *Pip* to keep clear of him[22]. A month later, *Drummle*'s time with *Matthew Pocket* is up and he leaves.

Chapter 27

Pip receives a letter from *Biddy* telling him that *Joe* is coming to London with *Wopsle* (who is embarking on a theatrical career there) and would like to visit *Pip* the following day. Interestingly, *Biddy* feels it necessary to lightly morally pressure *Pip* into accepting *Joe* - somebody he should have been delighted to see. She is right - *Pip* is disturbed by the prospect and relieved that *Joe* will come to *Barnard's Inn*, not *Matthew Pocket*'s home. In his usual way, he manages to excuse his embarrassment to himself. *Pip* has been wasting money on constant re-decoration of the *Barnard's Inn* apartment and made an ill-advised choice of a boy-servant for himself, who he calls the *Avenger*. The next day, the *Avenger* shows *Joe* in. He is very enthusiastic and happy to see *Pip*, but mad nervous by *Pip*'s awkwardness. *Herbert* returns home and is much more friendly and relaxed towards *Joe* than *Pip*, but the stressed *Pip* is glad when *Herbert* leaves for work. *Joe*, as when he visited *Miss Havisham*, speaks in a rather over-elaborate style and calls *Pip* 'Sir' to *Pip*'s annoyance. *Joe* is clearly not at ease out of his own small comfort zone of his home village. *Joe* then relates how *Pumblechook* told him that *Miss Havisham* would like to see him. On arriving, she asked if he is correspondence with *Pip*, and to tell him that *Estella* was home from overseas and would be glad to see him. *Pip* immediately becomes gladder to have seen *Joe* at this news, but *Joe* has got the message, says that divisions between people must always come and says he won't visit *Pip* again, though he'd always be welcome at the *forge*.

Chapter 28

Pip decides that he must leave for Kent the following day, and stay with *Joe*. After a visit to *Matthew Pocket*, however, he starts to find reasons why it would be better to stay at the *Blue Boar* in the same town as *Satis House*. The older *Pip*, as narrator, is hard on the younger *Pip* for this, though it could be argued that *Pip* needed to cut the blacksmith's apron strings, so to speak. He would take the two o'clock coach for Kent. Being winter, it would be long dark on his arrival at the *Blue Boar*. As was the practice, the coach party were joined by two convicts and their keeper. Interestingly, when a fellow passenger complains about the presence of the convicts, *Pip* has more sympathetic feeling for them than he shows for *Joe* - further evidence perhaps that his problem with *Joe* is to do with his closeness to him not *Joe*'s position in life as such. *Pip* recognises one of the convicts as the man who gave him the money in the *Three Jolly Bargemen*, although the man doesn't recognise *Pip*, now grown up and dressed as a gentleman - *Pip* is relieved, nonetheless, when *Herbert*, who has come to see him off, calls out goodbye to '*Handel*', not '*Pip*'. *Pip* dozes on the coach and wakes to hear the convict talking to his fellow about the incident with the two pound notes. He tell him that another convict had asked him, when he was released, to give them to a boy who had helped him once. The other convict had been tried again for jail-breaking and made a lifer. Irrationally afraid of being recognised, *Pip* decides to get out as soon as they reach the outskirts of town and walk to the Blue Boar, but all his old childhood fear stays with him as he walks. The waiter recognises him and asks if he would like him to send for *Pumblechook*. Surprised when he says 'no', the waiter shows him a newspaper article talking glowingly about *Pumblechook* as the oldest friend and mentor of the local boy - *Pip* - who had come into a fortune.

Chapter 29

Pip rises early the next morning and takes a walk in the surrounding countryside, reviewing his future prospects (which he apparently believes to be totally under the control of others). *Miss Havisham* had adopted *Estella*, and good as adopted him. It seems clear that she must intend that he inherit the house, which he is to restore, and marry *Estella*. Though he believes himself aware of the nature of her character, he knows that he can't get her out of his mind. *Pip* the narrator regards this as the key to what follows: he loves *Estella* because she is irresistible - against reason, hope, happiness and against all discouragement. When he rings the bell at *Satis House* it is answered by *Orlick*, who has left the forge and now works there as gatekeeper and security man. Briefly encountering *Sarah Pocket* on the way, *Pip* goes to the dressing -room where he first met *Miss Havisham*. She is there, accompanied by an elegant young lady who, rather surprisingly, given the circumstances, *Pip* doesn't immediately recognise as *Estella*. When he does, he feels once more like a 'coarse and common boy' in her presence, and how inaccessible she is. *Miss Havisham* asks *Pip* with a 'greedy look' if he found *Estella* much changed - clearly wanting him to be totally hooked. He knows that his feelings about her are hopelessly mixed up with all his dreams and aspirations, and he cannot separate her from what he calls 'the innermost life of my life'. Sent out to walk together in the garden, *Estella* admits to *Pip* to having watched his boxing match with *Herbert* and enjoyed seeing *Herbert* soundly beaten[23]. *Pip* says that they are now friends, and *Estella* replies that his new circumstances require new companions, that the company he had kept was no longer fit company for him now. This puts paid to any lingering chance that *Pip* might even visit *Joe*, let alone stay with him. *Estella* tries to warn *Pip* that she has no heart, that it's not she loves somebody else, it's that she's incapable of love. Just for a moment, he sees something - he calls it a ghost - something he recognises in her in her that he can't put his finger on, but it goes immediately.[24] Back indoors, *Pip* is informed that *Jaggers* is visiting and will join them for dinner. *Miss Havisham* is in her wheelchair in the wedding cake room. She starts on *Pip* again asking if he admires *Estella*, and launches into a frighteningly intense exhortation to love *Estella* however she treats him. She was adopted and educated to be loved - but, *Pip* notes, in *Miss Havisham*'s mouth the word sounds like a curse, not a blessing[25]. *Jaggers* has entered during this scene and *Miss Havisham*, on seeing him, composes herself. Privately, *Jaggers* tells *Pip* some more disturbing facts about *Miss Havisham* - she will never let anyone see her eat - she wanders the house at night and takes food then. *Pip*, clearly still troubled by questions of *Estella*'s identity, asks what her surname is - but of course it is Havisham[26] - she was legally adopted. *Jaggers* and *Pip* and *Estella* are joined for dinner by *Sarah Pocket*, whom a generally reticent *Jaggers* nevertheless goads, in his way, with *Pip*'s expectations which she, like the other members of her family, believe to be at her expense. Over a game of whist after dinner, it is arranged that *Pip* will meet *Estella* when she comes to London. *Pip* sleeps badly in the *Blue Boar*, troubled again by his infatuation for *Estella* that she did not reciprocate - and *Pip* the narrator is justifiably hard again on his younger self's feeling ashamed of *Joe* because of her.

Chapter 30

The next morning *Pip* tells *Jaggers*, who also spent the night at the *Blue Boar*, that he does not consider *Orlick* trustworthy enough for his job. *Jaggers* agrees and says he will pay him off. Fearing a meeting with *Pumblechook*, *Pip* leaves early on foot, asking the coachman to pick him up on the way. Worse than *Pumblechook*, however is the boy employed by *Trabb* who mercilessly mocks *Pip* all the way down the street to the amusement of onlookers[27]. Outraged, *Pip* writes determines to write to *Trabb* and withdraw his business[28]. As the town recedes he is again pricked by his ingratitude to *Joe* and, on arrival in *London*, sends *Joe* a 'codfish and a barrel of oysters' as a penitence. *Pip* confides his feelings about *Estella* to *Herbert*, who had already guessed as much. *Herbert*, like everybody else, assumes that *Pip* owes his fortune to *Miss Havisham* and that *Estella* is thus certainly intended for him and, if that is the case, all his agonising is like looking a gift horse in the mouth with a magnifying glass. Maybe everything will become clear soon, on *Pip*'s coming of age at twenty-one. *Herbert* cautions, however, that *Estella* is not a condition of the inheritance: otherwise *Jaggers* would have made that clear. He asks if *Pip*, if he is not bound to her, cannot then detach himself. *Pip* cannot: she is too much entwined with all his hopes and aspirations. *Herbert* then announces that he is secretly engaged to be married to *Clara*, a girl his snobbish mother would not approve of but who he intends to marry when he starts to make money. Rummaging through his pockets, *Pip* comes across the playbill that *Joe* gave him. The play is to be performed that night.

Chapter 31

Pip the narrator describes an inept rendering of Hamlet during which *Wopsle* was rudely heckled. *Pip* and *Herbert*, though sorry for *Wopsle,* can't help joining in the laughter. They decide to make a quick exit after the show, but are waylaid by the dresser, who tells them that *Mr Waldengarver* wants to see them. In the dressing room, they find *Wopsle*, known to the company by the stage name *Waldengarver* waiting for them. He asks how it went, in particular his performance. *Herbert* answers politely and *Pip* parrots his answers. *Wopsle* suspects the heckler was employed by the actor playing Claudius[29] They invite *Wopsle* back for supper, and he stays until two o'clock in the morning reviewing the performance and developing plans for the future.

Chapter 32

Sometime later, *Pip* receives a letter from *Estella* telling him that she is to arrive in London by coach at mid-day the day after next, and he is to meet her as arranged. When the day arrives, *Pip* is unable to settle, and gets to the coach station five hours early for fear of not being there.[30] *Wemmick* passes by on his way to work, and invites *Pip* to join him on a visit to *Newgate*. *Pip*, still anxious about deserting his post, nevertheless goes along. *Wemmick* is popular with the prisoners - being described as like a gardener among plants - but also some of the awed respect in which *Jaggers* is held has rubbed off on him. He negotiates a pair of pigeons out of a condemned prisoner who has no further use for them. When *Pip* arrives back at the coach station, he is still three hours early. He muses on how he keeps coming across convicts and crime, and thinks with horror of the difference between *Estella* and *Newgate*, whose taint, he fears, still hangs about him. Again, when he sees her, the 'nameless shadow' of some subconscious recognition passes fleetingly before him.

Chapter 33

Estella is more delicately beautiful and more winning in her ways than ever. She tells *Pip* that she is bound for *Richmond*, south of *London*. *Pip* is to take her purse and pay for refreshments while they wait for the coach - 'we have no choice, you and I... we are not free to follow our own devices.'[31] They go into the rather grubby hotel where they are brought all sorts of unappetising cakes and the like in addition to the tea *Pip* orders for *Estella* and overcharged. *Estella* asks about *Matthew Pocket* and talks about how his relatives hate *Pip* and try to harm him[32]. She laughs 'excessively' at this as if seeing them thwarted is one of the few pleasures open to her: she had grown up with them pretending to be sympathetic to her but plotting against her[33] When *Pip* kisses her hand she implores 'will you never take warning?' - of course he won't. On the way to *Richmond*, *Estella* looks eagerly about -she has never been to *London*, just passed through on the way to *France*. *Pip* points out *Matthew Pocket's* house as they pass through *Hammersmith*. *Estella* informs *Pip* that it is part of the plan that he should visit her 'when you think proper'. They part at the door of the house where she is to stay with an old friend of *Miss Havisham* - from before she withdrew from the world. *Pip* knows that he is never happy with her, but cannot be happy without her. He stops off at *Matthew Pocket's* house wanting to talk to him, but he is out.

Chapter 34

Pip continues to delude himself about the negative effects of his expectations, but wonders at times if he wouldn't have been better off if he'd never met *Miss Havisham*. But as he can't imagine life without *Estella*, it just goes round in circles. His lavish habits are having a bad effect on *Herbert*, leading him into expenses he can't afford. *Pip* himself is beginning to accumulate debt. Despite all this, when *Startop* suggests that they put themselves up for election to a club for young gentleman with too much money and not enough to do called the *Finches of the Grove*, they do so. The sole purpose of the club seems to be dining expensively and quarrelling, and the first member they encounter is *Bentley Drummle*. In short, *Herbert* has got nowhere in his search for capital and swings between ridiculous optimism and despair while *Pip* keeps himself busy between *Matthew Pocket*'s lessons, visits to *Richmond* and time at *Barnard's Inn* spending more money than he can afford and making out he's happy when he's not. From time to time *Pip* and *Herbert* would gather up their accounts, having fortified themselves with an expensive dinner, and go over their finances, confusing this with dealing with them. This self-indulgent floundering is briefly interrupted by a letter from *Trabb* & Co announcing the death of *Mrs Joe* and requesting *Pip* to attend the funeral.

Chapter 35

Pip feels little tenderness towards the sister who had done little to deserve it, but he feels a violent indignation against her attacker. *Trabb* & Co are acting as funeral directors and have staged an elaborate display of mourning[34]. *Joe* looks uncomfortable dressed as the chief mourner but also genuinely grieving. *Pumblechook* is serving refreshments, and the *Hubble*s are part of the mourning group. *Pip* notes that *Trabb*'s boy is not there. *Joe* had wanted a simpler less formal funeral, but was advised it would appear disrespectful, and the arrangements do appear to meet with the approval of on-lookers. *Mrs Joe* is laid to rest next to her (and *Pip*'s) parents in the churchyard where the story began. After everyone else is gone, *Pip* sits down to supper with *Joe* and *Biddy* and *Pip* asks if he can sleep in his old room. Later, *Pip* and *Biddy* talk. *Biddy* will have to leave, it not being seemly to stay alone in the house with an unmarried man. She will stay with *Mrs Hubble* and try for a job as a school-mistress at the new school. *Pip* asks *Biddy* about the death: *Mrs Joe* had seemed a little better and died quite unexpectedly, but had time to call for *Joe* and said *Pip*'s name too. *Pip* asks if *Orlick* is still about (he's still suspected of being *Mrs Joe*'s attacker) and is told he is working at the quarry - and still slouches about watching her. *Biddy* tells *Pip* how *Joe* loves him, and never complains about anything he does - the implication being that in her opinion he would be justified if he did. *Pip* says he will be down to see *Joe* often but *Biddy*, who often knows him better than he knows himself, doubts this, much to *Pip*'s annoyance. He feels she has done him an injustice. Early the next morning, as he leaves for the coach, he looks in on *Joe*, already at work, and repeats his assurance of visiting soon and often, which *Joe* receives good part. *Pip* rather self-righteously tells *Biddy* he is not angry, just hurt - she replying that if she is being unkind the hurt should be all hers. But of course, as *Pip* the narrator concedes, she is quite right.

Chapter 36

Pip gets further into debt, but both he and *Herbert* believe that when he soon comes of age, at twenty-one, even if he doesn't come into his expectations then, at the very least, *Jaggers* will give him more information. He makes sure that the date is well known around *Jaggers'* office. And sure enough he is summoned to be there at five o'clock on the afternoon of his birthday. The month is November. *Jaggers*, rather than making an announcement, asks I if has any questions. *Pip* asks if the name of his benefactor is to be made known to him that day, and is told no. He is however given a £500 banknote[35] to mark his coming of age and told that he will have £500 a year allowance until his benefactor chooses to appear. He can draw £125 a quarter, but beyond that *Jaggers* will exercise no control. He does not know when the benefactor will make themselves known to *Pip*, but his (*Jaggers*') role will end at that point. *Pip* invites *Jaggers* to dine with *Herbert* and him that evening at *Barnard's Inn*, which *Jaggers* accepts. While *Pip* waits for *Jaggers* to tidy up the day's business (and wash his hands), he asks *Wemmick* for his advice on helping a friend (he does not mention *Herbert* by name) who wants to start in business but needs capital. *Wemmick* answers that he might as well throw his money away - that is his opinion - in that office. *Pip* understands what he means by this - that the home *Wemmick* might take a different view - and asks if he might pay a visit to the *Castle*.

Chapter 37

The following Sunday, *Pip* goes to see *Wemmick* at home. The *Aged Parent* tells *Pip* that *Wemmick* is out but will soon be back, so *Pip* talks and nods to the deaf *Aged*. When *Wemmick* returns, it is in the company of a *Miss Skiffins*. *Wemmick* takes *Pip* out to see the garden in winter, giving *Pip* the opportunity to put his case to *Wemmick* at home. *Pip* knows he has not been good for *Herbert* financially - leading him into spending more than he can afford, and wishes his financial good fortune to benefit *Herbert* also, to the tune of £100 per year, to buy him into a partnership. *Pip* takes care to flatter *Wemmick* as one knowing how to do these things and *Wemmick* promises to think about it. *Miss Skiffins'* brother is an accountant and agent, and *Wemmick* will talk to him. They return to the house where *Miss Skiffins* makes tea while the *Aged* toasts bread at the fire. After tea, the *Aged* reads aloud from the newspaper while *Wemmick* tries several times to put his arm around *Miss Skiffins*, but it is always gently but firmly removed. *Pip* leaves early so that *Wemmick* can walk *Miss Skiffins* home. Later that week, *Wemmick* details a plan to *Pip*. There is a young merchant, or shipping broker, called *Clarriker* who has recently set up in business and needs intelligent help and capital for his business, with a view to the help eventually becoming a full business partner. The situation sounds ideal, and *Pip* pays down £250. *Skiffins* (the brother) conducts the negotiations so that *Herbert* suspects nothing of *Pip*'s involvement. *Pip* the narrator regards this as a turning point in his life, one where his expectations had finally done some good.

Chapter 38

Chapter 38 sees *Estella* begin to free herself of *Miss Havisham*'s control, but not in the way that *Pip* might want. *Pip* visits *Richmond* and takes *Estella* out frequently but is aware of her having many other suitors and feels that she uses him to make them jealous without ever actually showing him any favour. When he complains, she exasperatedly asks him if he will never heed her warnings about having no heart. One day, she tells *Pip* she must go to *Satis House* and asks *Pip* to go with her. He finds *Miss Havisham* 'more dreadfully fond' of *Estella* than ever, and she asks again 'how does she use you, *Pip*?' She then asks *Estella* to repeat the names and social positions of all her suitors (which *Estella* has told her in letters). *Pip* finally realises at this point that *Estella* has been sent to wreak revenge on men for *Miss Havisham*'s betrayal. He still, however, manages to believe that *Estella* is still destined for him after this revenge has been satisfied. For the first time *Pip* witnesses a fight between *Estella* and *Miss Havisham*[36]. It starts when *Estella* frees herself from *Miss Havisham*'s grasp, and *Miss Havisham* asks her if she's tired of her. *Miss Havisham* flies into a rage at *Estella*'s cool response, accusing her of having a cold heart. *Estella* coolly replies that she is what *Miss Havisham* made her. *Miss Havisham* gave her everything that she has, and she owes everything to her - but she cannot return what she was not given - and that is love. *Miss Havisham*'s reply shows that she can no longer (if she ever could) distinguish between love, jealousy and pain. But, *Estella*, continues, when has *Miss Havisham* found her unfaithful to what she has been taught? *Miss Havisham* accuses *Estella* of being proud, and *Estella* asks again who taught her. *Pip* leaves the room, signalling to *Estella* to help the distraught *Miss Havisham*, now collapsed on the floor. He walks outside for an hour and returns to find *Estella* sitting at *Miss Havisham*'s knee. *Pip* and *Estella* now play cards for *Miss Havisham* as they used to as children - only now it is sophisticated 'French games.' *Pip* is given a bed in the separate house in the grounds that *Herbert* stayed in, but can't sleep. At two in the morning he gets up and goes to the main house where he sees *Miss Havisham* walking along a passageway with a candle making 'a low cry'. The argument is never mentioned the next morning, or resumed on any of four subsequent visits. Much to his distaste, *Pip* the narrator returns now to *Bentley Drummle*. It is *Drummle*'s turn to propose a toast to a lady at a *Finches* dinner and he chooses *Estella*. *Pip*, thinking it is done out of spite towards him, challenges him with not knowing her. The *Finches* give *Drummle* a day to obtain proof and *Pip* must apologise if he does. The next day *Drummle* brings a letter in *Estella*'s handwriting confirming his claim, and *Pip* is forced to apologise. He finds it harder than ever to think that *Estella* should show favour to *Drummle* of all people, but indeed sees him behaving like the *Spider* that *Jaggers* calls him - patiently biding his time. *Pip* challenges *Estella* about this. At first she tries to brush it off, but he persists, saying that he can't bear to see her throwing herself away on such a man. She asks *Pip* is he wants her to deceive and entrap him - *Pip* can't see that she is showing she cares about him more than the others by not trying to deceive him - but of course he won't believe she can't love him and it's love, not consideration, that he wants.

Chapter39

Time has passed, and *Pip* is twenty-three years old. He and *Herbert* have moved to nicer lodgings at *Temple*. *Pip* has completed his education with *Matthew Pocket*, and can't settle to anything, which he attributes to uncertainty about what plans have been laid for his future. *Herbert*'s work is progressing, and he is away in *Marseilles*, leaving *Pip* alone, dispirited and anxious -which is not helped by the wet and stormy weather - the wind shaking their top-floor apartment. Many of the street lamps and the lights in the passage outside have blown out[37]. At eleven o'clock, as he is finishing his reading for the night, *Pip* hears a footstep on the stairs. He opens the door and enquires if anybody is there, and a stranger answers that he is looking for Mr *Pip*. When he says that's him, the stranger seems glad to see him and asks to come in. *Pip*, understandably, is not very welcoming but the stranger presses on in a friendly way before asking him if he's alone. Looking at him properly, *Pip* finally recognises him as the convict he helped as a young boy. The convict says that he's never forgotten how *Pip* acted all those years ago. *Pip* rather stiffly says that he hopes that he has shown his gratitude by mending his ways, and though the convict has come a long way to see him he has no wish to renew their chance relationship. *Pip* softens a little, and offers him some refreshment before he goes. Responding to a polite enquiry, the convict tells *Pip* how he's become a sheep-farmer and stock-breeder in the New World and has done wonderfully well. He asks *Pip* if he got the money from the man in the pub, which he had sent him. *Pip* tells him that it was a small fortune for a young boy, but now he has done well himself, and he returns the two pounds - which the convict sets fire to. The convict asks *Pip* how he has done well, and leads him slowly to see the truth - that it is he, the convict, who is behind *Pip*'s great expectations. The convict excitedly presses home his case, how he swore to himself that any money he made would go to *Pip* and how fortune favoured him, making him very wealthy. *Pip*'s reaction, far from gratitude, is one of horror, though fortunately the convict is too excited by his tale to notice. He tells how he prospered and how he made the perilous journey to see *Pip*. When hearing that *Herbert* shares the apartment, the convict urges caution, saying that he faces the death sentence if caught[38], having been deported for life. After the convict has gone to bed (in *Herbert*'s room) *Pip* sits up late into the night, thinking. He realises that if *Miss Havisham*[39] is not responsible for making him a gentleman, she cannot have intended *Estella* for him - he was just a puppet for *Estella* to practice on. *Pip*'s guilt at the way he has behaved towards Joe and his childhood terror of the convict all rise up in him again and falls into a troubled sleep in the sitting room. When he awakes, the candle and fire - his light and warmth - are burned down and out.

GREAT EXPECTATIONS CHAPTER SUMMARIES

Italicised words can be found in the lists of **Named Characters** or **Places**

Part 3

Chapters 40-59

Part three takes *Pip* from a twenty=three-year-old who has just discovered the truth about his Great Expectations to a man in his mid-thirties - the time at which the fictional narrator appears to be writing the book. In it we see the falling apart of all *Pip*'s expectations - which were largely outside of his control - and the maturing of *Pip* into a man who is less self-indulgent and more self-reliant. The ending of the book suggests that he is finally rewarded for his lifelong infatuation with *Estella*.[40]

Chapter 40

Pip wakes up before dawn worrying about how he will keep *Provis* from being discovered. He has a couple of gossipy women who clean for him, so he decides to put it out that *Provis* is his uncle, visiting from the country. On his way to get a light from the watchman (his candle has burned down while he slept) he falls over a man couching on the stairs, who does not answer when challenged. On returning with the watchman, the man is gone. At breakfast, under questioning from *Pip*, *Provis* says that his real name is *Abel Magwitch*. He is not well known in *London*, *Pip* is relieved to hear, but was tried there, which is how he met *Jaggers*. *Magwitch* repeats with obvious satisfaction how good it is to see *Pip*, but *Pip* is not pleased to see him, and feels repelled by him. *Magwitch*, not noticing *Pip*'s lack of enthusiasm, starts telling him how he must have horses and servants - he takes out a bulging wallet and gives it to *Pip* saying all he has is *Pip*'s. Asked how long he will stay, he says he is not going back. They discus where he will stay and how he will be disguised. *Pip* convinces him to dress as a prosperous farmer, and finds some rooms nearby for him to stay in. While out shopping for the clothes, *Pip* drops in at Little Britain, where *Jaggers* is careful not to be told anything about *Magwitch*'s presence in England, but confirms that a *Magwitch* in *New South Wales* is indeed *Pip*'s benefactor. He also mentions that somebody from the colonies called *Provis* wrote to *Wemmick* from *Portsmouth* asking for *Pip*'s address. The details of the correspondence with *Magwitch* and remainder of the cash in *Jaggers*' possession will be sent to *Pip*. *Magwitch* continues to show immense pride in *Pip*.[41] For the next five days, until *Herbert* returns, *Pip* does not go out (except to take *Magwitch* on night walks) for fear of missing him. When *Herbert* returns and finds *Provis*, *Provis* immediately drops any objections to *Herbert* knowing the real situation, but swears *Herbert* to secrecy on the Bible[42].

Chapter 41

Pip tells *Herbert* the whole story of *Magwitch* and sees that *Herbert* shares his feelings about it. *Pip* and *Herbert* can't wait to get *Magwitch* back to his lodgings so they can talk, but he doesn't leave until midnight. When they are finally alone, *Pip* tells *Herbert* that he doesn't want any more of *Magwitch*'s money and would repay what he'd already had if he could. His attitude seems to stem mainly from the realisation that the money is not from *Miss Havisham*, and therefore his expectations do not include *Estella* - he moans that he has been bred to no calling and is unfit for anything except becoming a soldier. *Herbert* points out that he'd never make enough money to pay anything back that way. *Pip* the narrator realises that even *Herbert*'s position is in jeopardy if he takes no more money. *Pip* now worries that *Magwitch* is a desperate character who has risked all to be there and might act in a desperate way and end up being arrested and executed if denied his dream of making *Pip* a gentleman.[43] *Herbert* argues that as long as *Magwitch* is in England, he has this power over *Pip* - they must find a pretext to get him out of England, and then *Pip* must break with him. When *Magwitch* joins them for breakfast that morning he is again full of plans for *Pip*'s future. *Pip* asks him about the fight with the other convict, and his life's story.

Chapter 42

Magwitch's earliest memories of himself are of stealing turnips in *Essex*. He never knew his parents. He was seen from an early age as a hardened criminal who was preached at a lot but not helped - his life became one of tramping, begging, thieving and working when he could. He was taught to read and write by fellows on the road. Over twenty years ago he met a man called *Compeyson*, and this was the man *Pip*, as a child, had seen him fighting in a ditch. *Compeyson* had been brought up as a gentleman, was good-looking and smooth-talking. He offered *Magwitch* work, though his work turned out to be swindling, forgery and money laundering[44]. He was heartless, cold and clever - good at getting others to do his dirty work while keeping himself at arm's length. *Magwitch* tells of how there was a man named *Arthur* lodging with *Compeyson* who was now ill but had once been in a very profitable scam with *Compeyson*, making a lot of money out of a rich lady. One night, when *Magwitch* was in the house, the feverish *Arthur* had come down from his room saying he was haunted by a woman - when he describes her, it is obvious she answers *Miss Havisham*'s description. In the early hours of the morning he cried out that she was coming at him with a shroud, and he died. *Compeyson* got *Magwitch* into debt and made a virtual slave of him. He was with *Compeyson* four or five years, picking up more convictions along the way, until they were finally charged together for using stolen banknotes. *Magwitch* sold his few possessions to pay for *Jaggers*, but *Compeyson*, the younger man, bought up a gentleman, was made out to have been led astray by *Magwitch*.[45] *Compeyson* gets seven years and *Magwitch* fourteen, *Magwitch* promising to smash his face if he ever meets him again. They ended up on the same prison ship (*hulk*) and *Magwitch*, attacked *Compeyson*, and was put in the ship's hold as punishment, from where he escaped. *Compeyson* then escaped out of fear of *Magwitch*, not realising he was also out. When the young *Pip* told *Magwitch* about the other convict, *Magwitch* went looking for him, and called the soldiers in order to get him returned to prison. Again, *Compeyson*, saying he's escaped out of fear of *Magwitch* was given a light sentence while *Magwitch* was sent way for life. That was the last *Magwitch* heard of Compeyson. *Herbert* passes *Pip* a note confirming that *Miss Havisham*'s half-brother was called *Arthur* -and *Compeyson* must be the mad who wooed and jilted her. They would not tell this to *Provis* (*Magwitch*).

Chapter 43

Thinking over what *Magwitch* has said, *Pip* realises that if *Compeyson* is still alive and discovers that *Magwitch* is back, he will inform on him for his own safety. *Pip* is more convinced of the urgency of getting '*Provis*' out of the country but, not knowing how long he himself will have to be away, wants to see *Estella* and *Miss Havisham* before he leaves. At *Richmond* he is told that *Estella* is at *Satis House*. He is puzzled, as she has always been taken by him before, but he resolves to go there. He takes the early morning coach the next day, and arrives at the *Blue Boar* in the drizzling rain only to see *Bentley Drummle* coming out. They pretend not to see each other and continue to in the breakfast room, until *Pip* can no longer bear *Drummle*'s hogging of the fire and joins him standing in front of it. A hostile conversation ensues with *Drummle* making mocking reference to little marsh villages and smithies - letting *Pip* know that he knows about his humble origins. He asks the waiter if his horse is ready, saying the lady won't be riding today in account of the weather, but he will be dining with her that evening - obviously goading *Pip*. His horse is brought round and *Pip*'s breakfast is served, but neither is prepared to make way at the fire until finally some rain-soaked farmers come in requiring it. Before *Drummle* rides off *Pip* sees him talking and joking with somebody who looks from behind like *Orlick*. *Pip* can't eat his breakfast but washes his face and heads off to *Satis House*.

Chapter 44

Estella is sitting at *Miss Havisham*'s feet in the dressing room, knitting, when *Pip* arrives. Both look up and *Miss Havisham* asks what has brought him. *Pip* miraculously intuits from *Estella*'s knitting action that she realises he has discovered who his benefactor is[46]. *Pip* confirms this, telling *Miss Havisham* that he is as unhappy as she could ever have intended him to be, and his real patron is not likely to do anything for his reputation or position in life. He throws accusations about letting him believe she was his benefactor at *Miss Havisham*, which she mostly refutes. He claims that she used him to spite her greedy relatives, but she should not include *Matthew* and *Herbert*, who are not greedy, in this. He asks if she might spare the money in secret to finish a work [the paying off of the partnership] which he has started in secret. She looks into the fire for a long time then asks 'what else?' Turning to *Estella*, *Pip* confesses that he's always loved her, though he knows now that she'll never be his. *Estella* says that she cannot feel love for anyone - she has tried to warn *Pip*, but he wouldn't listen; but is a mark of the esteem in which she holds him that she tells him even that much. *Pip* then confronts her with his knowledge that she is dining with *Drummle*, insisting that she cannot love him. She exasperatedly asks him what she has just told him - but she is to marry *Drummle*. This is her decision, not *Miss Havisham*'s, and it is because he is a man unlikely to be hurt by her lack of love. *Pip* says he cannot bear it - she has always been at the heart of his being. He leaves with *Estella* staring incredulously after him and *Miss Havisham* looking wracked by pity and remorse. He walks all the way back to London[47], arriving home after midnight, but the night porter hands him a note in *Wemmick*'s writing saying 'Don't go home.'

Chapter 45

Pip takes a cab[48] the *Hummums* hotel in *Covent Garden* and spends a sleepless night there. He realises he must see *Wemmick* before he transforms into his work self, and sets out for the *Castle*, arriving at eight 8.00am. *Wemmick* tells *Pip*, in his careful lawyerly way, that word had reached *Newgate* that *Magwitch* had left *New South Wales* and that *Pip* had been watched. *Wemmick* confirms that *Compeyson* is alive and in *London*. He has spoken to *Herbert* about moving *Magwitch*, and *Herbert* has taken him to the place where his intended wife, *Clara*, and her ailing father lodge. There was a spare room to let there. *Herbert*, who visits frequently, can act as a go-between. *Wemmick* suggest that *Pip* visit *Magwitch* at his new lodgings before going home and again urges him to secure the 'portable property' (in this case money) as anything could happen to *Magwitch*. *Pip* spends the day at the *Castle* with the *Aged*, then leaves after dark to see *Magwitch*.

Chapter 46

After a certain amount of trouble finding the place, *Pip* finally arrives at *Mrs Whimple*'s house, where *Magwitch* is now staying. *Pip* has not met *Clara* before, and *Herbert* has warned him she doesn't regard *Pip* as a good influence on *Herbert* due to his spending habits. *Pip* however instantly likes her, and is sure she is right for *Herbert*. *Pip* and *Herbert* go upstairs to see *Magwitch*. *Pip* has decided not to tell him that *Compeyson* is in town for fear that he'll go looking for him, but tells him the rest of what *Wemmick* said, emphasising how important it was to get out of England. *Herbert* has been thinking that he and *Pip* are both good rowers, and could take *Magwitch* someway down the river from where they could board a ship headed for the continent. *Pip* could keep a boat at the *Temple* stairs and practice regularly so it did not attract attention when he set out. *Magwitch*'s room overlooks the river, so he can pull down his blind whenever *Pip* passes as a signal that all is well. *Magwitch* is known at the establishment as *Mr Campbell*. So *Pip* and *Herbert* leave separately and meet up again at the *Temple* apartment. The next day, *Pip* buys a boat and he starts taking it out regularly, sometimes with *Herbert*, sometimes alone, and in all weathers. He slowly extends his range to *Erith* in Kent. *Herbert* continues to visit *Clara* and to see *Magwitch* with no worrying news, but *Pip* can't shake the feeling of being watched.

Chapter 47

Weeks pass with little change. *Pip* is waiting for a sign from *Wemmick* that it is safe to take *Magwitch* down the river. He still does not want to take any more money from *Magwitch*, despite *Wemmick*'s advice. He returned *Magwitch*'s wallet, and now has to sell jewellery for ready cash. It is an unhappy time of uncertainty for *Pip*, both about when he will make his escape with *Magwitch*, and whether *Estella* is yet married. Rather than spend the evening alone after returning from a row one foggy day, he goes out to the theatre. *Wopsle* is still there, but now acting bit parts. He spots *Pip* in the audience after which *Pip* notices him staring in his direction whenever on stage. As *Pip* leaves, *Wopsle* catches him and tells him he had recognised the person sitting behind *Pip* as one of the convicts fighting on the marsh many years earlier, now dressed prosperously. As casually as he can, *Pip* confirms that he means the one who was being beaten - *Compeyson*. After a drink with Woplse, *Pip* gets home late and writes to *Wemmick*, reminding him they are waiting to hear from him. Going to post it, he again looks for somebody following him, but sees no-one. Nevertheless, he decides he must keep well clear of *Magwitch*.

Chapter 48

About a week later, *Pip* is strolling around Cheapside looking for somewhere to eat when he is stopped by *Jaggers*, who invites him back for dinner. *Wemmick* is there, but not his Walworth self, hardly acknowledging *Pip* and focusing his attention on *Jaggers*. *Pip* is handed a letter from *Miss Havisham*, who didn't know his address and wants to see him about the business he discussed with her on his last visit. He takes *Wemmick*'s lack of objection to going the next day as a signal that the coast is not yet clear for springing *Magwitch*. *Jaggers* confirms that *Estella* has married Drummle and proposes a toast to her then calls Molly, commenting on her slowness that day. Looking at her eyes and hair and the motion of her fingers, and remembering the strange feelings he has experienced, *Pip* is sure that Molly is *Estella*'s mother. *Pip* leaves with *Wemmick* who quickly regains his Walworth personality. He admits that much as he admires *Jaggers* he knows he can't be himself in his presence. *Pip* asks *Wemmick* what he knows about Molly. He says that she was up for murder at the Old Bailey about twenty years ago and *Jaggers* got her off - it was the case that made his name. She was accused of strangling another woman out of jealousy over a tramping man she was in a common-law marriage[49] with. The prosecution claimed that she had also killed the three-year-old child that she had had with the man out of revenge for his unfaithfulness, but *Jaggers* pointed out that she was not being tried for that. She had been in his service ever since.

Chapter 49

Pip leaves for *Satis House* by the early coach, breakfasts at the *Halfway House* Inn and walks the rest of the way so as to enter the town quietly. It is afternoon when he arrives, and the gates are opened by an elderly servant. He finds *Miss Havisham* in the room with the long table, sitting staring into the fire and looking very lonely. She asks how much he needs to buy *Herbert's* partnership and *Pip* replies that £900[50] is required. She writes an authority for *Jaggers* to pay *Pip* this money on *Herbert's* behalf. She then asks *Pip* if, when he feels he can, he will write that he forgives her. He says he has already done so and that he is too much in need of forgiveness himself to deny it to her. *Miss Havisham* drops to her knees, crying out time and again 'What have I done?' She is able to see the terrible effects of the working out of her revenge on the innocent people - children especially -who got caught up in it, but unable to translate her anguish into trying to put things right (beyond the easy bit of paying out the money for *Herbert*). *Pip* is now mature enough, however, to react with compassion, and says she need have no regrets on his behalf, it is *Estella* who is the one most hurt. *Miss Havisham* says all she'd wanted at first was to protect *Estella* from the hurt which she herself had endured, but she sees now how she stole her heart and put ice in its place. *Pip* replies that a natural heart, even if bruised or broken, is always better - but he has felt compassion for *Miss Havisham* ever since he first heard her sad story, on his arrival in *London*. He asks her about *Estella*, and *Miss Havisham* confirms that *Jaggers* found and brought her to *Miss Havisham*, who had asked him for an orphan she could adopt, when she was 2-3 years old. *Pip* leaves, wanting to take a last look at the house and its grounds. He again sees the vision he had as a child of *Miss Havisham* hanging from a beam in the old brewery, and decides he had better check she is all right before finally leaving. He sees her sitting by the hearth, but as he is about to leave, her dress catches fire and she runs shrieking at him engulfed in flames. He throws his heavy coat and the table-cloth over her to put out the flames. She is unconscious as the servants arrive, and help is sent for. He continues to hold her until the doctor arrives and is surprised, when he finally releases her, to see that his own hands and arms are burned. The doctor says that *Miss Havisham's* burns are serious but not life-threatening, though there is still a danger from the nervous shock. She is laid on the table, inevitably reminding *Pip* of how she had said she would be when she was dead. *Pip* makes arrangements for *Estella* and the Pockets to be told what's happened. When *Pip* leaves for home early the next morning *Miss Havisham* is delirious, endlessly repeating her sense of guilt and need for forgiveness.

Chapter 50

Pip's burns to his hands and left arm, though dressed by the doctor and again be *Herbert* are very painful, and will prevent him from rowing for some time. *Herbert* reports that he talked to *Magwitch* for a couple of hours the previous evening, and all is well. In fact, he is much more likeable and very chatty. He talked about a young woman who he'd been in a relationship with who had been very jealous and vengeful. She had been tried for the murder by strangling of another woman and *Jaggers* had successfully defended her, which is when *Magwitch* had first heard of *Jaggers*. This woman and *Jaggers* had had a child who *Magwitch* was very fond of, but she had told him she was going to kill the child on the same day as the other woman was killed, to punish *Magwitch*. He had never seen the child again, and never saw the woman again after she had been arrested. All this happened about twenty years ago. The child was a girl, and *Pip* tells *Herbert* what he is now certain of: that *Estella* is *Magwitch's* daughter.

Chapter 51

Not sure what to do with the information about *Estella's* parentage, *Pip* decides to seek *Jaggers'* opinion. He is please to find that *Wemmick* is also present as they are doing the accounts. First, he tells them about *Miss Havisham's* accident, and then produces the authorisation to draw £900 on

Herbert's behalf. *Jaggers* expresses regret that there is nothing for *Pip*, and he says (much to *Jaggers'* and *Wemmick*'s incredulity) that he was offered money and refused. Getting onto the subject of *Estella*, *Pip* tells them that, unlike *Miss Havisham*, he knows who her mother is - and unlike *Jaggers*, he knows who her father is: *Provis*[51], from *New South Wales*. Noting *Jaggers'* attempt to hide his surprise, *Pip* tells the whole story of how he knows (implying he got from *Herbert* what he actually got from *Wemmick*). *Jaggers* tries to close the subject down, so *Pip* appeals to *Wemmick*, saying, much to *Jaggers'* amazement, that he knows he has a tender heart, and has seen his aged father and playful ways. Recovering from his astonishment, *Jaggers* relents as far as to tell his part in *Estella*'s story in hypothetical terms. He tells how a legal advisor might have been asked by a rich lady to find her a girl to adopt and how, having seen the evil that so many children fell into, might have thought he could save one from that fate - and how he might have taken the mother into his own care. Suppose the child grew up and married for money, and both parents were still alive, and living near each other, but none of the three knew where the others were or if they were still alive: would any of them be better for the knowledge?[52] They all agree not to tell any of those involved and *Jaggers* and *Wemmick* return to their accounting.

Chapter 52

Pip takes the cheque drawn on *Miss Havisham*'s account to *Skiffins*, who brings *Clarriker* to *Pip*, and the agreement is concluded: *Herbert* is a full partner. *Pip* the narrator reflects that this was the one good thing that he had done since hearing of his expectations.[53] *Clarriker* says that the business is doing well and they will soon need *Herbert* to run an office in the East.[54] *Pip*'s left arm was slow healing and when, in March[55], the letter arrives from *Wemmick* saying they should go ahead and take *Provis* overseas, he is still unable to row. *Herbert* suggests that *Startop* can take over *Pip*'s role as rower. *Pip* says they should get well down river, past *Gravesend*, then hail and board a steamer heading for the continent. The steamers would leave at high water, so they should row down on the previous ebb tide. *Herbert* goes off to recruit *Startop* and *Pip* to get passports for himself and *Provis*[56]. They meet up, plans are laid for the day after next, and *Pip* goes home alone, where he finds a grubby anonymous not addressed to him, saying that if he wants information about 'Uncle *Provis*' he must go to the old sluice by the *lime kiln* on the marshes at 9.00pm that or the following night. He is not to tell anybody. Worried that it be something important to *Magwitch*'s safety, he leaves *Herbert* a note saying he is going down overnight to see how *Miss Havisham* is before he goes overseas, and rushes to catch the coach. He avoids the *Blue Boar*, taking supper at a smaller inn, then visits *Satis House* where a servant at the gate tells him that *Miss Havisham* is still very ill. Back at the inn the landlord, not knowing who he is, regales him with his own rags to riches story and *Pumblechook*'s starring role in it, and of the ingratitude of the young man in question. The narrator *Pip* notes how *Joe*, to whom he had shown genuine ingratitude, had never complained to anyone. When the time comes, *Pip* heads out for the sluice house.

Chapter 53

It is a dark night, but *Pip* knows the marshes well. The *lime kiln* by the quarry is still burning, but the workmen have gone home. There is a light in the dilapidated old sluice house. *Pip* knocks, but there is no answer, so he goes in. He calls, but there is no answer, so he goes out to look, then back in, when he is attacked from behind, knocking the candle out. The next thing he knows his arms are pinned to his sides by a noose thrown over him and pulled tight. The pain to his burned arm is excruciating. A voice says 'Now I've got you!' as he is tied to the loft ladder and threatened not to call out. As the candle is re-lit, he recognises *Orlick*[57] as his attacker. *Orlick* tells *Pip* how *Pip* has always been in his way - at the forge, losing him his job with *Miss Havisham*, getting between him and *Biddy* - and now he is going to get *Pip* out of his way permanently by killing him and throwing his body in the lime kiln, so nobody would ever know what had happened to him. *Pip*, at that moment, is more worried about all the people - *Joe, Herbert, Magwitch*- who will remember him as having deserted them, than he is of dying. He resolves to die resisting, not pleading for mercy. Believing *Pip* will die as he intends, *Orlick* tells *Pip* that it was indeed he who had attacked *Pip's* sister, *Mrs Joe*. It was *Orlick* who *Pip* fell over on the staircase at the *Temple* - when he lost his job, thanks to *Pip*, he had taken up with new masters - forgers. *Orlick*, already a little drunk, drinks from a flask, getting more reckless. He says he knows who *Provis* is: it was his leg-iron he attacked *Mrs Joe* with, and he knows *Pip* is hiding him - but his new master is cleverer than *Provis* - when *Pip* is out of the way he will come for *Provis*. He mentions the name *Compeyson*. He then picks up a stone hammer and starts towards *Pip* who shouts and struggles with all his might. He hears an answering shout - figures rush in and *Orlick* flees. *Pip* finds himself unbound on the floor and sees *Trabb's boy*, then *Herbert*, then *Startop*. *Herbert* explains that in his hurry he dropped the note from *Orlick*, which *Herbert* read and realised something was wrong. The rushed down after him and followed his trail, picking up *Trabb's boy* (now a young man) as a guide. *Herbert* is all for reporting *Orlick* to the magistrate, but *Pip* fears that they might have to stay there and miss their appointment with *Provis*. *Pip* rests up the following day and wakes at dawn on Wednesday feeling fit and strong. They set out at 9.00am as the tide turns.

Chapter 54

Pip had no idea where he would end up or when he would be back, but his only concern was for *Magwitch's* safety. The tide would be on the ebb for six hours until 3.00pm, but they would keep going, against the tide, until after dark when they would put in at a waterside inn and spend the night there. Steamers for *Rotterdam* and *Hamburg* would leave by the next morning's high tide, and they would hail and board whichever appeared first. *Magwitch* boards, as planned, at *Mill Pond Bank*. *Pip*, who is steering, keeps an eye open for any sign that they are being watched, but sees none. They make good progress, and the tide is still ebbing as they pass *Gravesend*. *Pip* steers out of the main channel as the tide turns, but the rowing is hard for *Herbert* and *Startop*, though they manage another four or five miles. They stop off at a dirty little public house which feeds them on bacon and eggs and provides two twin rooms for the night. A local asks them if they've seen the four-oared galley going up and down the river. Concerned about this, *Pip* confers with *Herbert* and *Startop*, but they decide that it's best to stick to their plan. However, in the night *Pip* sees two men looking at their boat then heading off across the marsh. They decide that *Pip* and *Magwitch* should walk a way up the shore and join the boat there if all was clear. So it goes, until the steamers appear at 1.30pm and the galley shoots out ahead of them. As the first streamer approaches, one of the men on the galley orders them to stop as they have a returned transport[58] on board. The galley pulls alongside, and *Magwitch* reaches over to pull the hood from a sitting figure, who is seen to be *Compeyson*. The steamer, whose crew have not seen what is going on, crashes into them, the other following close behind. *Pip, Herbert* and *Startop* are rescued quickly, but *Magwitch* and *Compeyson* have disappeared. Finally *Magwitch* is seen, swimming, and pulled on board and manacled. He is injured in the chest and on the head by the steamer paddles, but there is no sign of *Compeyson* who was locked in a fight with *Magwitch* as they went overboard. *Magwitch* has to hand over all possessions, including the wallet full of money to the officials on the boat. As *Pip* watches *Magwitch* in the boat he at last fully appreciates what he has done and is glad in a way that his injuries will probably prove fatal so that he is spared public hanging. *Magwitch* does not realise that all his remaining property will be forfeit to the crown and *Pip* will have none of it. He thinks it has all been worth for *Pip* to be rich, and *Pip* doesn't tell him this won't be the case. *Pip* promises to stand by him as long as he lives.

Chapter 55

A guard from the prison ship is sent for to identify *Magwitch* as *Compeyson* is confirmed dead. *Pip* goes to *Jaggers* who says it is an open and shut case - there is nothing to be done for *Magwitch*. He again reprimands *Pip* for letting the fortune slip through his fingers: there is apparently nothing in writing making *Magwitch*'s remaining wealth over to *Pip*, and as he is not related to *Magwitch*, he has no claim[59]. He decides not to even contest the issue, though there is a list found on *Compeyson*'s body of *Magwitch*'s property and bank accounts which corresponds to a list given to *Jaggers* by *Magwitch* of what was due to *Pip*. *Magwitch*'s trial is set for one month's time. *Herbert* tells *Pip* what *Pip* already secretly knows, that he must leave for an office in *Cairo*. He is sure that he will need a clerk, and *Pip* might be able to work up to being a partner. *Clara* says *Pip* would be welcome to stay with them, when they are married. *Pip* thanks them be says he can't see beyond the next few months, where he will be spending as much time as possible with *Magwitch*. *Herbert* leaves for *Cairo*. Later that week, *Pip* runs into *Wemmick* who feels guilty about his mistake regarding *Compeyson*. *Compeyson* had appeared to be away, and this seemed like a good time to attempt the escape. He doesn't think that *Magwitch* could have been saved, but the 'portable property' (money) might have been. He announces that he is to take a holiday the following Monday and asks *Pip* if he will join him for a morning walk. *Pip* agrees and goes to the *Castle* as arranged. *Wemmick* goes through an elaborate game of pretending to make chance observations that lead him into a church where he is married to *Miss Skiffins* with *Pip* as best man. *Pip* leaves after an excellent wedding breakfast promising that the wedding will not be mentioned in *Little Britain*.

Chapter 56

Magwitch is unwell in prison - he has two broken ribs and a wounded lung. Breathing is painful and difficult, so he can't talk much, but *Pip* talks to him and reads to him. He is moved to the prison infirmary where he not shackled and *Pip* has more opportunities to talk to him, but he continues to get weaker. Despite knowledge amongst the staff of his reputation he is 'humble and contrite' to all, slowly winning them over. *Jaggers* applies for a postponement of the trial in the hope that he will die before he faces the court, but it is refused.[60] The trial is short as the facts are incontrovertible - that he has done well is *New South Wales* is not relevant: he is sentenced to death[61]. While still hoping that *Magwitch* will die before the sentence is carried out, *Pip* gets to work petitioning the Home Secretary and others for mercy saying *Magwitch* had come back for his sake, not his own. While searching *Pip* to make sure he is not carrying poison[62], the infirmary staff reassure him each day that *Magwitch* is worse and when, ten days later, he is clearly on the point of death, they allow *Pip* to stay with him until the end. *Pip* tells the dying man that his daughter is still alive, she is very beautiful, and he loves her. *Magwitch* kisses *Pip*'s hand and dies. *Pip* prays for mercy for his soul.

Chapter 57

Now free to leave, *Pip* gives notice on the tenancy of his *Temple* apartment. He knows his money situation is bad, but lacks the energy and focus to deal with it. Soon all the stress of the last few months catches up with him and he falls into a delirious fever. He remembers odd incidents, like two men in his room saying he was under arrest for debt, but is too weak to respond. Slowly as the tide of the illness turns he becomes aware of *Joe*'s presence with him, but isn't really able to engage with the reality of the situation until the end of May[63]. *Joe*, it appears, has been there nursing him all that time - told by *Biddy* go at once on hearing about his illness. *Biddy* has apparently successfully taught *Joe* to write, and they have been in correspondence all the time *Joe* has been away. *Miss Havisham*, *Pip* is told, never recovered and died about a week after *Pip* was taken ill. The bulk of her estate went to *Estella*, but *Matthew Pocket* received four thousand pounds as a result of *Pip*'s intervention.

Sarah, *Georgiana* and *Camilla* got derisory sums. *Orlick* is in prison after breaking into *Pumblechook*'s house. *Joe* continues to care for *Pip* who is still very weak, and they spend a lot of time talking. *Pip* notices, however, how as he grows stronger *Joe* becomes more uneasy with him, as if he is only able to relate to him in a caring role: *Pip* is shocked when, as he first walks by himself again, *Joe* calls him 'Sir'. *Pip* realises that as he became rich he increasingly pushed *Joe* out of his life and *Joe* is (perhaps subconsciously) expecting the same again as he grows stronger. *Joe* departs in the night while *Pip* is asleep, leaving a receipt for the debt for which *Pip* was arrested. He has paid it off out of his meagre savings. *Pip* had already been planning to go to see *Biddy* to show her how humble and repentant he was and ask her to marry him, as if to prove it. He now resolves he must follow *Joe* home to carry out his plan. He sets off three days later.

Chapter 58

News of *Pip*'s change of fortune has preceded him and he is no longer treated like an important guest at the *Blue Boar*. He sees that the contents of *Satis House* are up for auction the next week and the house is to be demolished. Returning for breakfast at the Blue Boar, *Pip* finds *Pumblechook* talking to the landlord. *Pumblechook* again harps on his role in *Pip*'s good fortune and *Pip*'s ingratitude, implying that his fall from that fortune is due to this moral failing on his part[64]. *Pip* leaves to see *Biddy* at the school, but finds it closed for the day. He goes on to the forge, which is also closed, though the house is open and decked with flowers. *Joe* and *Biddy* emerge arm in arm, having just been married. Both are overjoyed to see him, and *Pip* is enormously thankful that he never told *Joe* of his plans, as he had meant to the morning after *Joe* left *London*. He says he must leave within the hour to join *Herbert* in Egypt, but will work hard to repay *Joe* the money used to clear his debts. He asks that if they have a son they don't tell him how unjust he was, but that their child will be a better person than him. He asks them for their forgiveness[65]. He returns to the *Temple*, sells what he can and negotiates repayment terms with his remaining creditors. Within a month he had joined *Herbert*, within two months he was a clerk, and within four months he had an opportunity to run the office alone as *Herbert* went home to marry *Clara*. It was many years before he became a partner, but he lived happily and frugally with *Herbert* and *Clara* and paid off all his debts, keeping up a correspondence with *Joe* and *Biddy* all the while. When *Pip* finally becomes a partner, *Clarriker* finally tells *Herbert* the secret of how *Pip* engineered and paid for his position, saying it had long been on his conscience. The business is never grand, but has a good name and all prosper. *Herbert* remains as cheerful and helpful as ever and *Pip* realises that he is not the inept dreamer he once took him for. He wonders if it had not perhaps been he who was inept all along.

Chapter 59[66]

Pip returns to see *Joe* and *Biddy* after eleven years overseas. One December evening he comes up to the house after dark and gently pushes open the kitchen door. *Joe* is sitting there smoking his pipe, a little greyer but otherwise unchanged[67]. In the corner by the fire is a young boy. His name is *Pip*. The next morning *Pip* the elder takes *Pip* the younger for a walk to the churchyard to look at the family graves. *Pip* asks *Biddy* if he can borrow young *Pip* sometimes but she says he must rather get married. *Pip* says he's too settled with *Herbert* and *Clara*, so *Biddy* asks if he isn't still pining for *Estella*, which he denies. *Estella* had separated from *Bentley Drummle* who had become notoriously cruel and brutal, and he had died two years previously in a riding accident caused by his mistreatment of his horse. *Pip* walks into town, arriving at the remains of *Satis House* at sunset, where, to his amazement he meets *Estella* looking sadder and older but still beautiful. It is the first time that she has been back to the house since she left it. *Drummle* has squandered her fortune and the ground is all she has left, kept from him by not being sold. She asks after *Pip*, showing some knowledge of and genuine interest in his life. She says she has thought of him often of late. She never thought, however that she would take leave of *Pip* in taking leave of *Satis House*. The memory of their last parting is painful to her, but if he could bless her then can he bless her now that she understands how he felt then, and part as friends. The narrator concludes his story by saying that he 'saw no shadow of another parting from her': he sees no reason for them to be parted again.[68]

THEMES:

Charles Dickens was, above all, a story-teller - so while he undoubtedly cared passionately about social justice and worked a lot of the wrongs in his society into his plots and characters, he does not give the impression of having sat down and said to himself "I'm going to write a book about Love", or "Loss", or "Greed" or whatever. It seems more that he had an idea for a story - a young orphan boy is lifted out of poverty by a benefactor and made a gentleman, for instance - then work out the circumstances of how and why it might have happened, find and flesh out the characters, and then look at the consequences for those characters. Although he would have known roughly where he was going with his story, his books were usually originally published in instalments in magazines, and he would undoubtedly have been influenced by the feedback he got along the way, building on characters that gripped the public imagination and occasionally introducing characters who hadn't been in the original plan to overcome a plotting problem. Having said which, of Dickens' fifteen novels, eleven take their title from a named individual or place and two titles (*A Tale of Two Cities* and *Our Mutual Friend*) reference an individual or places in the story. It's only *Hard Times* and *Great Expectations* which seem to refer specifically to a theme, so we should perhaps start with the theme of *"Great Expectations"* itself before looking at other themes which Dickens explored to a greater or lesser extent in the novel.

Note: *there are no set names for the themes in a novel, so your teacher may have used other words to describe the same idea [some are given here as 'also known as], but the themes in Great Expectations fit roughly into these categories:*

Main Theme: '*Great Expectations*'

Dickens wrote the book as if the autobiography of Pip, so as far as Pip is concerned his '*Great Expectations* ' were the core theme of his life up to the age of writing in his mid-thirties. Indeed the book starts when he is seven years old and contains next to nothing about his life prior to that - and it does so because this is when he first meets Magwitch, the man responsible for his change in fortune.

However, this is not a simple fairy-tale about an orphan child who does a good deed to a poor man and is rewarded enormously when that man becomes rich and lives happily ever after: it is much more complicated than that. But to explore this as a theme we need to be clear that the title and the central chunk of the story are about the expectations of wealth, not the wealth itself.

It's frustrating not to know more about Pip's parents as he is clearly a very intelligent child well able to benefit from a gentleman's education - but this is not to say that the effects of his change of circumstances are entirely benign: while he is in the process of transformation he is very unfair to and unappreciative of Joe and Biddy - this might have been psychologically necessary but it's not admirable!

The real significance of Pip's expectations however is that they weren't just about money - and the condition of coming into his fortune that he must make no attempt to discover who his benefactor is leads to a confusion which allows him to believe that Estella, whom he been infatuated by almost since he met her, is intended for him. So there are two threads: in one he helps a convict on the marsh who wants to give Pip what he could never have for himself - he wants to make him a gentleman; in the other, quite independently, a rich, jilted spinster uses him in grooming her adopted daughter, Estella, to take revenge on men and in the process Pip gets a taste for the life of a gentleman and a desire to become one in order to have a chance of winning Estella. When these two threads come together they get hopelessly entangled in Pip's mind, so that his expectations are not just of wealth, but of Estella too. When Pip believes that his life is mapped out for him, that he is going to receive a large portion of Miss Havisham's fortune with Estella thrown in for good measure, he loses control of his own life and direction, over-spending even his generous allowance and finding no purpose. His better nature starts to fight back when he begins funding Herbert's business partnership, but it is only when he discovers the true source of his expectations and is appalled by it and the implications of it that he starts to make good decisions. Although Wemmick and Jaggers are horrified by the ultimate forfeiture of Magwitch's wealth to the British state, Pip had decided long before then that he didn't want the money - he even wishes he could pay back what has already been spent on him. What he finds hardest to come to terms with is the realisation that if the money didn't come from Miss Havisham, then Estella is not intended for him.

So there is a subtle play on words going on between the more archaic meaning of "expectations" as prospects or inheritance, and the now more common meaning of a belief that something will happen. Pip is given expectations in the older sense and builds his own (in the newer sense) on them - at the cost of a lot of heartache and distress. **[Information like this will also count as contextual information in an exam.]**

But neither expectation is ever realised (although Dickens implies, in the revised ending which became the published one, that Pip might finally get together with Estella after the end of the story as written): they are vapour - and as long as he looks to his expectations rather than his own resources to give his life purpose, he flounders. When he says no to the money, when he accepts that Estella is lost to him, then he can start putting things right: he can make Miss Havisham value her cousin Matthew and his son Herbert, he can appreciate Joe and Biddy for what they are -and he can set about earning his own living in a respected business. None of this would perhaps have been possible without meeting Miss Havisham and Estella or Magwitch's and Miss Havisham's money, but they were never ends in themselves. Miss Havisham build her life on a dream and threw it away when the dream didn't work out; Magwitch dreamed a dream of making a poor young orphan a gentleman, and this dream gave him the motivation to turn his life around - but he too had no Plan B when things didn't turn out like he'd expected - in fact he refused to recognise it. Miss Havisham's various relatives, Sarah Pocket, Camilla and Georgiana waste much time and effort on the expectation of a share of Miss Havisham's fortune. Even Matthew Pocket expected life to fall into his lap as, to some extent, does his son Herbert. Orlick expected to be apprenticed by Joe and becomes murderously bitter when he is not. Expectations are all very well, but they should never be relied on - that, perhaps, is the main theme of the story. There are, of course other themes that are woven through the text and are important in realising the objectives of the story.

Some related themes running through the story are: Control; Growing up; Society; Love; Crime; Time.

You may get a question about the significance of the title, which will enable you to explore the theme more fully, but it is more likely that Pip's expectations would be mentioned in the extract and you'd be asked about how those expectations are realised in the novel as a whole, or to what extent his expectations are met/ are great/ are expected etc.

Theme: Control

As a boy, Pip is chiefly controlled by Mrs Joe and Pumblechook. In Part 1, mostly round the Christmas meal in Chapter 4 and the visit to Miss Havisham in Chapter 7 & 8, we see how they keep putting Pip in his place, telling him how grateful he should be that his sister has 'brought him up by hand'. She uses her cane, ironically called 'Tickler', to control both Joe and Pip and this is what Pip is expected to be grateful for. In Chapter 2 Pip is beaten for being out at the cemetery too long – which is where the convict found him: *'My sister, Mrs Joe, throwing the door wide open, and finding an obstruction behind it, immediately divined the cause, and applied Tickler to its further investigation.* **She concluded by throwing me -- I often served as a connubial missile -- at Joe**, *who, glad to get hold of me on any terms, passed me on into the chimney and quietly fenced me up there with his great leg'.* The way she throws Pip at Joe illustrates her control of him, and we're told this happens 'often'.

Then, when he pretends to have eaten his bread quickly in order to hide it for the convict, she takes control again: *'My sister made a dive at me, and fished me up by the hair: saying nothing more than the awful words, "You come along and be dosed."'* The phrase, *'fished me up'* emphasises Pip's passivity.

Constant reminders of what a miserable baby he was, how horrible little boys are and how great her sacrifice in bringing him up has been, keep Pip 'beholden' to her. She calls herself **'a slave with her apron never off'**, but that is another way of exerting control.

When Pip is teaching Joe to write [chapter 7] and he warns Pip they need to keep their scholarship a secret lest Mrs Joe suspect an uprising, and explains his own enduring of her bullying:

`Stay a bit. I know what you're a-going to say, Pip; stay a bit! I don't deny that your sister comes the Mo-gul over us, now and again. I don't deny that she do throw us back-falls, and that she do drop down upon us heavy. At such times as when your sister is on the Ram-page, Pip,' Joe sank his voice to a whisper and glanced at the door, `candour compels fur to admit that she is a Buster.'*

Joe pronounced this word, as if it began with at least twelve capital Bs.

`Why don't I rise? That were your observation when I broke it off, Pip?'*

`Yes, Joe.'*

`Well,' said Joe, passing the poker into his left hand, that he might feel his whisker; and I had no hope of him whenever he took to that placid occupation; `your sister's a master-mind. A master-mind.'*

`What's that?' I asked, in some hope of bringing him to a stand. But, Joe was readier with his definition than I had expected, and completely stopped me by arguing circularly, and answering with a fixed look, `Her.'*

`And I an't a master-mind,' Joe resumed, when he had unfixed his look, and got back to his whisker. `And last of all, Pip -- and this I want to say very serous to you, old chap -- I see so much in my poor mother, of a woman drudging and slaving and breaking her honest hart and never getting no peace in her mortal days, that I'm dead afeerd of going wrong in the way of not doing what's right by a woman, and I'd fur rather of the two go wrong the t'other way, and be a little ill-conwenienced myself.*

So, by keeping her apron on, Mrs Joe reminds Joe of his *'poor mother, of a woman drudging and slaving and breaking her honest hart and never getting no peace in her mortal days,'* and so keeps him *'dead afeerd of going wrong in the way of not doing what's right by a woman'* .

This quoted explanation could be the extract chosen for a question about Joe's character, Joe's relationship with Mrs Joe, Pip's relationship with Joe as well as a question on the actual theme. It is more likely that you will need to mention the theme as one of the things you notice in the extract than that you will be asked about the theme specifically. Remember also to mention contextual information like at the time a woman was expected to run the household.

Later in that same chapter Mrs Joe and Pumblechook have arranged that Pip will sleep in town at Pumblechook's in preparation for his visit to Miss Havisham – notice that he is never clearly told what is happening, much less consulted. Again he sister treats him like and object: *'…she pounced upon me, like an eagle on a lamb, and my face was squeezed into wooden bowls in sinks, and my head was put under taps of water-butts, and I was soaped, and kneaded, and towelled, and thumped, and harrowed, and rasped, until I really was quite beside myself. (I may here remark that I suppose myself to be better acquainted than any living authority, with the ridgy effect of a wedding-ring, passing unsympathetically over the human countenance.)'*

Pumblechook exerts control not only by promising Pip's services to Miss Havisham, but by getting him to do arithmetic under time-pressure. Once Pip has 'expectations' he changes tack immediately and tries to control him through false humility, asking over and over whether he may shake Pip's hand. Later still, he suggests that it is thanks to him that Pip has any expectations at all, exaggerating both his role and his care of Pip in introducing Pip to Miss Havisham [see Chapter 28].

If you are asked a question about the theme of 'control' you might be given a passage from Part 1 in which someone is controlling Pip and you'll need to pick out the sort of quotes as above, but there is not time to go into that much detail when you're talking about the theme in the novel as a whole. Depending on the actual question, you may also want to mention briefly other examples of control.

Magwitch tries to make Pip into what he wants him to be. Although he means it for good, he doesn't pause to think that he might be alienating Pip from his family, friends and trade. When he returns to England, he takes it for granted that Pip will be delighted to see him and will look after him. [See Chapters 40 & 42]

Miss Havisham tries to make Estella into somebody to carry out her revenge. She trains her up to treat men with disdain, using her beauty as a weapon to break their hearts. She gives Estella 'great expectations' sending her to finishing school and leaving her a fortune, even though her mother was a murderess and her father a convict. She tries to make Pip fall in love with Estella from the start and when he is an adult continues to encourage him to love her [see Chapter29]. However, Estella does not submit to her control indefinitely and by chapter 38 begins to show Miss Havisham just how cold her heart is.

Estella tries to control her relationships with people. She gives them just enough attention to fall in love with her and then keeps them at arm's length. She tells Pip that she has chosen to marry Drummle because he is so cold hearted that she won't hurt him [Chapter 44] and that Pip is the only one she has not tried to deceive. When Pip kisses her hand the first time they're alone in London, she begs 'will you never take warning?' [Chapter 33], because she does not want to hurt him.

Jaggers controls Wemmick (he is a totally different person at work to at home) and everybody else, including Estella's mother, Molly [see Chapter 26].

Compeyson exerted control over Magwitch by drawing him into more crime, taking a cut, but leaving him to face the consequences [See Chapter 42].

Theme: Growing up aka Bildungsroman [*about the moral and psychological growth of the main character*]; growing pains.

Great Expectations is Pip's story, and the main story takes him from seven years old to twenty-three to twenty-four years old: it's a story about the passage from childhood to adulthood. This isn't the main theme, however: there are gaps in the narrative at times that might have been significant. The three parts are of approximately equal length, yet Part 1 takes Pip from seven to eighteen, Part 2 from eighteen to twenty-three, and Part 3 takes place within a year (with the exception of Ch. 59).There is a lot more which is glossed over or rushed through in Part 1 than the others, though this encompasses the crucial 'growing up' years. So the focus isn't on Pip's growing up *per se*, but it is on how a series of external events- and the way he responded to them as he grew up- shaped his life.

The focal points in his development are meeting the convict, Magwitch; meeting Miss Havisham and Estella; being released from Joe and going to London with 'great expectations ' to become a gentleman; being ashamed of and so neglecting Joe and Biddy and all that reminds him of his origins bar Miss Havisham; patiently pursuing Estella in the belief that she is 'meant' for him by Miss Havisham; meeting Magwitch again and having his hope that Estella is part of his 'expectation' dashed; confronting Miss Havisham and forgiving her; beginning to do good for others: getting Miss Havisham to 'do something' for Herbert, trying to save Magwitch, visiting him in prison and being reconciled with Joe and Biddy and finally, Estella.

The adult Pip is quite scathing about the young Pip's ingratitude and dissatisfaction about his station in life, which gives the reader a sense of just how far he has come. One could say he has moved from being a gentleman in the material sense of wealth and status, to being a gentleman in personality, like Joe and Herbert are.

A typical question on this theme could be the opening scene from Chapter 1 as your extract and then asking you to consider to what extent the novel is about Pip's search for a father [this really is a question that has been asked before]. Another question might be about what makes a good person, given that this is Pip's journey to becoming a better person. For such a question the extract might be when Joe nurses Pip back to health after Magwitch has died.

Theme: Society aka social standing, culture, class, wealth; 'ambition vs accepting your lot'; 'motivation to better yourself'; 'we are who we are'; 'what makes a gentleman'; 'hopes, dreams & plans'.

The Victorian era was one of both social mobility and one where you were expected to accept the position in life that God had obviously ordained for you. A hymn written at the time summed it up as: *The rich man in his castle,/ The poor man at his gate, /God made them high and lowly,/ And ordered their estate.* At the same time, many educated people were organising night schools where they taught labourers to read and 'self-help' was encouraged. These contradictory stances are explored in the novel.

What makes somebody a gentleman is a very strong theme in *Great Expectations*. Pip wishes to be a gentleman when he is exposed to how the other half lives at Satis House - and more particularly as he becomes infatuated with Estella - he knows he has no hope first of not being looked down on by her, and then of winning her, if he is not a gentleman. So what is a gentleman? There seem to be three components, though perhaps only two of them are necessary: breeding - being born the son of a gentleman; fortune - having a source of income sufficient not to have to work directly for it; education and manners.

Drummle is born a gentleman, has the income of a gentleman, but he is but stupid and ill-mannered. Breeding and fortune, however, are sufficient to qualify him as a gentleman.

Herbert is born a gentleman and has the education and manners of a gentleman, but no fortune. He needs, ultimately to work for a living, but qualifies as a gentleman.

There are other gentlemen - **Matthew Pocket** is in a similar position to his son, Herbert; **Startop** seems, from what we are told, to qualify on all three counts. **Arthur Havisham** was born a gentleman [though his mother was 'low born' being a servant], but disinherited of his fortune and was lacking the manners so he fell from his position. **Compeyson** seems to be someone who adopted the persona of a gentleman but had neither the breeding not the fortune - nor, in fact the behaviour, though he could put it on to charm people. **Pumblechook** aspired to be accepted in polite society, but had neither the breeding nor the fortune - nor, in fact the manners, despite his affectations - to be a gentleman.

It's clear that **Pip**, when we first meet him, has none of the attributes of a gentleman. He has some advantages - he is intelligent and able to learn, his sister and Pumblechook are (admittedly for self-interested reasons) keen that he should better himself, and Joe is a gentle man - not a vital trait, as Drummle shows, but one normally considered desirable. Pip receives a rudimentary education at the village school, but learns about what money can do for and to people from his visits to Miss Havisham. When given a large living allowance and schooled as a gentleman, he is accepted easily into society -in strong contrast, for example to Jane Austen who's characters, though living at roughly the same time as Pip, demonstrate and experience a lot more snobbery regarding their breeding. In fact, the biggest problem Pip has is not with being accepted as a gentleman by that social class (with the exception, as always, of Drummle, who taunts him with his origins), but with those who already knew him: Joe goes into a very deferential mode, the shopkeepers become obsequious, and Trabb's boy is downright rude. Other servants, like the Avenger, also sense that Pip doesn't have the natural authority that comes with being born into wealth, and are not very respectful of him.

Estella has an even lower birth than Pip - the (in the legal sense) illegitimate daughter of a jailbird involved in a forgery racket and a vagrant woman of violent temper who threatens to murder her daughter and (we are led to assume) actually murders a love rival. However, nobody except Jaggers knows her parentage (and he only knows who her mother was), and she is legally adopted by a wealthy heiress and brought up as a lady, and her status as such is never challenged.

Joe has no interest in being of a higher social class, he feels secure in 'the old work', yet in his code of behaviour he is more of a gentleman than most – he and Herbert are counterparts on either side of the social divide.

Magwitch is an interesting case with regards to class. He has such a terrible start in life that he doesn't even know who his parents are or how he got his name. He was shunned by society, preached at rather than fed when he stole food, and his life was one of vagrancy and petty crime interspersed with periods in prison. However, he always tried to better himself - he learned to read and write from fellow vagrants, and when given the opportunity for a new start in New South Wales he seized it with both hands and prospered remarkably.

A typical question on this theme may be based on the time Joe visits Pip in London and says, *"I'm wrong in these clothes. I'm wrong out of the forge, the kitchen, or off th' meshes. You won't find half so much fault in me if you think of me in my forge dress, with my hammer in my hand, or even my Pipe"*, showing the prevailing attitudes to class and asking you to consider how Dickins explores class in the rest of the novel. Or you may be set the scene where Herbert is helping Pip learn table manners and then be asked to consider the novel as a whole and say to what extent you think Herbert is the only true gentleman in the novel.

Theme: Love aka 'love & loyalty', love & friendship'

Despite the richness of the English language, it's strange that the word love has to cover so many different relationships, from sexual love to brotherly or sisterly love, to mother-child love, to a love of humanity in general - and that's without even starting on things you might love doing or possessions or pets you might love. So, there are many relationships in *Great Expectations* which might be described as love, some of which are major strands in the storyline, but as love can take many different forms it's worth looking at those which are more important to the story one at a time. Other relationships, such as that of Herbert's parents, though we see them in some detail, are not really significant to the movement of the plot or character development.

One-sided relationships:

Pip & Estella - Pip's unrequited live for Estella is a central thread running through the story. He wants to become a gentleman because of her; it is to see her that he keeps going to Satis House long after Miss Havisham has paid for his apprenticeship to Joe; he is caught up in a limbo of waiting and dancing attendance on her rather than getting on with his life partly because he believes that she is part of his 'expectations'; he goes through emotional trauma due to her inability to love him and his inability to accept it; he never marries, even when she is married and he believes himself over her.

Pip & Biddy - it is very clear in their teenage years that Biddy is attracted to Pip but, partly blinded by his infatuation with Estella (and, it has to be said, that Estella is beautiful and Biddy is plain) and partly because he needs her as a friend and sees her as an older sister, he fails to notice. When, after Estella has married Drummle and Pip has suffered a nervous collapse from which he is nursed back to health by Joe, he finally decides that she is for him, they are both lucky that she is already married to Joe by the time he comes to tell her: she has a good man who shares her moral code, and he is spared a marriage that would never make him truly happy.

Pip & Joe - Although Joe is twenty-two years Pip's senior Joe retains a lot of child-like qualities and his relationship with the orphaned Pip, to whose sister he is married and who he has taken into his care is more like that of an older brother than that of a father. Joe's love for Pip is unwavering, always looking out for him and wanting what's best for him. Pip's love for Joe starts strong - he sees him as his only friend as a child - then wavers as he feels the need to break away from the life Joe represents and is embarrassed by him in the company of the type of people he aspires to be, but comes back strong at the end when Pip has suffered enough to appreciate Joe's steadfastness and decency.

Joe & Mrs Joe - An interesting relationship in which there is clearly some love and attraction on Joe's part, though Pip could see nothing attractive about his sister, and she treats Joe with a certain contempt. A possible answer would be that she had been unable to look after Pip properly and Joe came to the rescue, but her gratitude turned to bitterness because of his lack of ambition. In the end, though, as she is dying, she does show him some affection - suggesting it was there once.

Magwitch & Pip - For all his roughness, Magwitch has quite a sentimental character and not only remembers the boy who helped him when he was an escaped convict, but wants to live out his dreams in that boy. His affection makes him blind to the initial revulsion that Pip feels for him when he reveals himself as his benefactor. Pip does eventually come to appreciate Magwitch after he has been jailed and then hospitalised.

Miss Havisham & Compeyson - The big love affair, on Miss Havisham's part, that occurs before Pip's story begins but profoundly affects the course of his life. Dickens is skilful in producing a psychologically convincing back-story for Miss Havisham: she is brought up without a mother and with a doting father who dies leaving her a large fortune, making her both a likely target for con-men and somebody who might well be naive and susceptible to charm. She is also at an age where it would be expected that women of her class would already be married. Compeyson, though younger than her, knows, with Arthur's help, what buttons to push, and there is no doubt that she was besotted with him. When she is jilted she is at first traumatised and then filled with a burning desire for revenge - not on Compeyson, but on men in general. (Without getting to psycho-analytic with a fictional character, she might also have had suppressed issues with her father for 'betraying' her by getting married again without her knowledge and even dying when she needed him.) This isn't the place for going into the effects of this flip side of passionate love on Pip directly and through Estella, but 'love gone wrong' is an important aspect of the theme.

Mutual relationships:

Pip & Herbert - In the days when it was not acceptable for unmarried men and women to live together it was common for young unmarried men to share apartments and have very intimate non-sexual relationships, and for men (or women) to talk openly about loving each other without any connotations beyond that of greatly enjoying each other's company and trusting each other with their true feelings about things - what we might call 'best mates'. In fact, as today, these relationships can be stronger than the man's relationship with his wife - as it often was in the personal life of Dickens himself. This was the sort of friendship that Pip and Herbert instantly struck up - they were not unaware of each other's faults, but their enjoyment of each other's company definitely qualified as a form of brotherly love.

Herbert & Clara - We don't get to know much about Clara other than that she disliked Pip before she met him, thinking (rightly) that he was responsible for Herbert living beyond his means (along, possibly, with a little jealousy) and that she and Herbert seemed made for each other - neither of them was as passionate a character as Pip and they were totally at ease in each other's company. In some ways Clara is little more than a plot device - appearing when Estella returns to England and moves to Richmond - her presence on Herbert's life might make Pip more aware of the lack of a woman in his own. The fact that Pip lives with Herbert and Clara after in Cairo after they are married but remains single himself highlights again that he is still in love with Estella and doesn't want anybody else.

Joe & Biddy - Joe is about twenty years older than Biddy and has known her since she was a child, so the relationship is not an immediate one, but they grow close to each in the time she is house-keeping for Joe after Mrs Joe has been attacked. While Biddy is a quick learner and Joe is uneducated, they both share a strong sense of right and wrong and the strength of character to stand by what they believe, so, in that sense, they are a natural couple. In fact, if the book was their story, it could be seen as a classic romance, full of setbacks and rivals but coming through at the end. Biddy also gives Joe the child that Mrs Joe never did.

Wemmick & Miss Skiffins - this is not a major storyline, but Wemmick is an interesting character in the way he splits himself between the rather cynical and pragmatically dry person at work and the whimsical person he is out of work. In his and relationship with and particularly his marriage to the very proper Miss Skiffins, he hides a rather romantic self behind a very unromantic facade. Miss Skiffins, like Clara, is to some extent a device to move Herbert's story in the required direction, but Dickens uses the opportunity to create yet another love relationship cameo.

Wemmick & his father - happy intergenerational family relationships are thin on the ground in *Great Expectations* , so Wemmick's mutually affectionate relationship with his father, the Aged Parent, is notable for that reason if no other.

Pumblechook & himself - it shouldn't strike us as in any way surprising that the comparatively prosperous Pumblechook appears never to have married because he is enormously self-centred, over-fond of his own opinions, willing to take credit where it's not due and offence where it's not warranted.

Magwitch & Molly - it's difficult to know, and we're not told, how good this relationship was. We do know that they regarded themselves as married by country custom, stayed together for several years, and had a child together. Magwitch seems to have largely written her out of his life after her trial and her threats to kill their child, and indeed his affections seemed to have wandered to another woman who became the intensely jealous Molly's victim, precipitating the trial. But if, as suggested, Estella got her looks from Molly then she must have been a very attractive young woman and she certainly felt strongly enough about Magwitch for her jealous rage to get the better of her. So we get the impression of a somewhat tempestuous relationship fuelled by sexual love if nothing else.

Mutually destructive relationships: (if Love is a theme, its absence is part of that theme)

Miss Havisham & Estella - about ten years after the trauma she suffered on being jilted on her wedding day, Miss Havisham, by then in her mid-thirties and apparently wishing to have nothing more to do with men (in anything other than a professional role, like Jaggers) decided she wanted to adopt a girl child as an object for her love. This might have been a good thing: having a young child in the house might have given Miss Havisham a better perspective on her life and allowed her to put the past behind her, had the child not been beautiful. As Miss Havisham saw the child becoming more beautiful, she started seeing her as a weapon of revenge against men - somebody who they would irresistibly be drawn to but she could make cold to their love - somebody who would do to men what she had had done to her by a man. Thus the relationship allowed her to maintain a focus on her own grievances and destroyed Estella's chances of a happy marriage - and possibly Pip's.

Estella & Drummle - Estella knows she is incapable of love and marries the stupid and brutish Bentley Drummle because she thinks he is too insensitive to notice. In doing show she actually shows a level of concern for others that is also act of defiance against Miss Havisham who wants her to go on causing misery to many suitors. In a strange way it is also an act of love towards Pip whose ardent love for her had somehow touched her: she knows he will not give up hope of her until she is married to someone else. In fact Estella suffers greatly for her choice of husband until she is relieved by his death - typically as a result of mistreating a horse. As Pip is an *unreliable narrator* - somebody deeply emotionally involved in the story he is (fictionally) telling, it's never possible completely to rely on his version of events but there is a suspicion that Drummle's motives for the marriage might have been partly to spite Pip. The marriage was doomed from the start, though Estella does emerge as somebody more in touch with her feelings.

Orlick & the World - We don't know much about Orlick's past - he seems to be introduced to the story in order to attack Mrs Joe and developed from there - but he seems to have a massive chip on his shoulder which puts him at odds with everybody he meets and sets him on a destructive path. In this he contrasts strongly with the gentle Joe Gargery, for whom he works when we first meet him, who sees good in everybody.

Questions on this theme are likely to include an extract featuring a set of these characters, like the description of Wemmick trying to put his arm around Miss Skiffins [chapter 37], then ask about how Dickens presents relationship/ love in the novel as a whole.

For context, remember that the majority of marriages were still arranged, though literature promoted marriage for love. Dickens himself was not allowed to marry the girl he loved, because her parents disapproved. Significantly, they ended the relationship by sending her to 'finishing' school in Paris, just as Miss Havisham sends Estella. Later Dickens married a girl he tried to love and had many children, but he actually cared more for her sister. Eventually, as a middle aged man, had a secret affair with an actress.

Theme: Crime aka 'crime & the law'; 'crime: guilt & innocence'; revenge; criminality; 'lies & deceit'.

Crime drives a lot of the story of *Great Expectations* - indeed in Ch. 32, Pip muses over how he keeps coming across criminals and crime. As with all themes we must remember that this is Pip's story, and themes are important only insofar as they impact of his life.

If we focus first on actual criminal behaviour and law enforcement, we can define three groups of people representing different aspects of the law featured in the story: these are the criminals, the law enforcers and the lawyers and judges. It's worth spending a moment seeing how these aspects affect Pip.

Criminals

Magwitch's first memory is of stealing. Up until his early thirties he was in and out of jail for petty crimes - mostly for survival as he was willing to work when he could. When he fell in with Compeyson he got involved in more serious organised crime. He was sent to prison for fourteen years, escaped and was deported. He put crime behind him and grew rich honestly in Australia, but then returned to England to see what he had made of Pip - this itself was in fact a crime as far as the law was concerned - his worst yet, punishable by death. So it was through crime that he met Pip, and because of his deportation that he was able to make the fresh start in a land of opportunity that made him wealthy enough to carry forward his dream of making Pip a gentleman.

Compeyson is a career criminal dealing in fraud and forgery in an organised way. Although he is a shadowy figure who we don't see or hear much directly in the story, his actions largely drive and shape the plot and Pip's life. It is his fraud on Miss Havisham that caused her to become like she was when Pip met her; it is he who lured Magwitch into organised crime and who left him to carry the take the bigger rap when they were caught. It was Magwitch's desire for revenge on Compeyson that got him deported (and in the end caused them both to die). It was quite possibly Compeyson's association with Orlick that led Orlick to try to kill Pip. In a sense, Pip is a bit player in a drama stage-managed by Compeyson, though, in the end, the story is Pip's story.

Orlick is a surly and resentful journeyman labourer who reacts violently when crossed. When Mrs Joe incites Joe to fight him in her defence (a fight the big, strong Joe easily wins) he comes back and attacks her in a cowardly way, leaving her brain damaged. He harbours resentments against Pip for (as he sees it) taking his place as Joe's apprentice, for (as he sees it) thwarting his attempts to woo Biddy and (more legitimately) losing him his job as Miss Havisham's gatekeeper. When he falls in with Compeyson, he follows Pip in order to track down Magwitch, who Compeyson reasonably enough sees as a threat, but then lures Pip to a meeting on the marshes and attempts to kill him. He is later arrested for breaking into Pumblechook's shop.

Others: Wemmick introduces Pip to various prisoners at Newgate who seem to be friendly and accept their fate - even hanging - with resignation.

Law Enforcers

We meet law enforcement agencies throughout the story, though the characters are seldom developed and never named. We first meet the prison guards who interrupt the Gargery Christmas meal in search of a blacksmith to mend their manacles when Pip is seven. Pip (with Joe and Woplse) accompany these guards as they track down escaped convicts (later revealed to be Magwitch and Compeyson). Some rather ineffectual police investigate the attack on Mrs Joe, staying around for some days but achieving nothing. There are prison guards present, naturally, when Pip visits Newgate with Wemmick, and Wemmick engages in a friendly way with them. Finally, there are the relentless and competent river police who apprehend Magwitch as Pip and friends try to row him to freedom, and the more kindly people guarding Magwitch at Newgate and then at the hospital where he dies.

Lawyers & judges

The legal system is most fully realised in the character of Jaggers, and to a lesser extent Wemmick, whose work and home personalities provide a sort of bridge between Jaggers and Pip. Jaggers is a lawyer through and through - very careful and precise and sometimes wary of committing to a position (though not afraid of expressing his own opinions where he disagrees with something) and happiest when dealing with points of law: indeed he seems to find the rather messy real world quite distasteful, washing it off before leaving his office each day. He is, however, the sort of lawyer who believes in doing things properly and in right and justice, and as such is a valuable formative influence to Pip with regard to behaving responsibly with his new found wealth. His legal career again impacts at significant moments on the story, just as Compeyson's life of crime does. Jaggers makes his name successfully defending the almost certainly guilty Molly, but takes her daughter, whom she has threatened to kill, away from her, giving her for adoption to the wealthy and childless Mss Havisham - the child of course being Estella. It is through this case that he comes to the attention of Magwitch - Estella's father, who employs him then and years later, employs him again as a go-between with Pip. It should be noted that Jaggers' considerable reputation and undoubted ability didn't do Magwitch much good on either occasion when he defended him. Pip also sees the justice system at work watching Jaggers in court in Chapter 24 and at Magwitch's trial in Chapter 56.

Pip is clearly worried as a child by truth and lies: he wants to be truthful, but the truth is often impossible due to fear of the consequences and the unsympathetic attitudes of the adults around him.

Also, there are a lot of things that would be illegal - or at least likely to provoke investigation - today which weren't then. For example, Estella would likely be taken away from Miss Havisham, Drummle's treatment of Estella (by all accounts) would probably get him into trouble, and his treatment of his horse certainly would have, if the horse hadn't 'taken the law into its own hands', so to speak.

Dickens was a reporter for a time, writing up court cases, so would have come across many criminals and the stories of their crimes. In addition, once wealthy he ran a home where prostitutes could be rehabilitated, learning useful skills enabling them to earn a better living. He would have heard their stories and known of their suffering. He used to go for very long walks in London and would also have come across many children begging.

Extracts like Magwitch and Compeyson fighting on the marshes in Part 1 or in the water in Part 3, or Orlick attacking Pip might set up a question on this theme, as might Pip watching Magwitch die or Jaggers in court. The 'whole novel' question could be to what extent the novel is about crime, or to what extent Pip is drawn into crime despite himself from the very start of the novel.

Theme: Time aka 'change vs stasis'

Any story takes place through time, and the main story of *Great Expectations* covers about seventeen years with another eleven years elapsing between the penultimate and final chapters. However, time does not affect all equally, and this is what makes time an important theme in this story.

Most of the characters in *Great Expectations* don't change much during the course of the story so, in a way, we see Pip, who does undergo great changes, navigating through a fixed landscape and learning to deal with it. Of course this effect is heightened because we don't have access to the internal life of any other character, but most characters don't change much, only Pip's perception of them changes as he himself changes.

Pip's circumstances change radically more than once: we first meet him as a poor orphan boy taken in as a son by his kindly brother-in-law and his rather less kindly sister; he then has to take the role of a playmate for the spoiled adopted child of an eccentric heiress, and becomes discontented with his life. Next, his visits are concluded and he has to revert to being an apprentice blacksmith, until released from this by a mysterious benefactor and the promise of 'great expectations'. He then lives the rather aimless life of a young gentleman waiting to come into his inheritance until meeting his benefactor, discovering to his horror that it is not Miss Havisham, which means that his relationship to Estella has not been plotted out towards their marriage, and that the man is an ex-con, whom the newly gentrified Pip looks on (ironically) with revulsion. The final transformation he makes is to decide that he doesn't want Magwitch's money, at which point he can start to repair the strained relationships in his life and take charge of his own future as an honest man of business.

Around Pip, as mentioned, the other characters mostly stay as they are and any change in their relationship with him is down to the changes in him. Although Pip exhibits some not very admirable character traits at times, particularly in relation to Joe and Magwitch, it is worth noting that the essentially good main characters (Joe, Biddy, Herbert, Wemmick, Jaggers) all like Pip, while the essentially bad main characters (Orlick, Drummle) don't like Pip. (Compeyson, though possibly the worst of the lot, has no significant direct interaction with Pip.) Main characters who have become bad through circumstances - (Miss Havisham, Estella, Magwitch) all grow better after interacting with Pip. Pumblechook is not malicious -just full of himself - and pursues self-interest, like the other traders of the town. The same is essentially true of the likeable minor characters with (in particular) Startop, Matthew Pocket, Clara (once she knows him) and Clarriker liking Pip while less likeable characters Sarah Pocket, Georgiana, Camilla & Raymond, 'the Avenger' and Trabb's boy, all for their own reasons, disliking him. From this we can read that Pip is essentially a good person who is knocked off course by events over which he has no control, but whose goodness reasserts itself as he takes control of his own life. Themes are interwoven to make the fabric of a story, but important point here is to see how these factors translate into Pip's development through time.

When answering any questions on any theme, it is always wise to mention changes in time. Say what has changed from the start of an extract to the end, how a character has changed within the novel or how events bring about change.

Many of the questions will not be specifically about a theme, but mention of a relevant theme being explored in an extract or implied in a question will improve your grade. For example, you may be asked how Dickens presents Pip in an extract and in the novel as a whole. You would consider how the events of the novel shape his development, exploring the things looked at under the theme 'Growing up aka Bildungsroman'. Any of the events mentioned in that section could be used as extracts for such a question.

Finally, remember that even though you won't be asked specifically to say anything about the times in which Dickens wrote the novel, or Victorian beliefs, or how ours differ, you will actually be expected to say something relevant about context, not as a separate add-on, but to explain a point. For example, if you were talking about Jaggers giving Estella to Miss Havisham, you could mention that there was no child welfare at the time, orphanages were overcrowded and cruel, and a girl like Estella would likely be left to beg on the streets or be sent to the workhouse, so although we would think what he did terrible today, in the context of the time he probably saved her life.

ABEL MAGWITCH

Aka: the convict, Magwitch, Provis, Mr Campbell

Biography:

Abel Magwitch would have been born in around 1768, eight years into King George III's long reign. Interestingly, 1768 was also the year in which James Cook's first expeditionary party set out: they were to be the first Europeans to set foot in Botany Bay which gave its name to the penal colony where the fictional Magwitch would be deported to years later. He would have lived through American independence from Great Britain and the Napoleonic wars, which didn't end until 1815, three years after he met Pip. It is unlikely that any of these great historical events would have had much direct bearing on his life, however, as he was always an outcast from society.

Although we meet Magwitch as 'the convict' right at the start of the story, he does not appear again until sixteen years later, in Ch. 39, when he introduces himself to Pip again as the source of his Great Expectations.

In Ch. 40, the first chapter of Part 3 of the novel, he describes himself as having been brought up to be a 'varmint' - and American corruption of vermin, meaning (in this context) a troublesome person - but it is not until Ch. 42 that he relates his life's story to Pip and Herbert (and us). He summarises it as *'In jail and out of jail, in jail and out of jail, in jail and out of jail. There, you've got it. That's my life pretty much, down to such times as I got shipped off...'*

He doesn't remember his parents, or even how he knows his name. His earliest memory is of stealing turnips in Essex. He quickly got a bad reputation and people were quick to morally censure him for stealing food, but not to give him food to eat or a way of earning money - a nice Dickensian touch. For all this, he did have an urge to improve himself and learned to read and write from men he met on the road. He continued in and out of jail and working when he could until the turn of the century when he was in his early thirties. This is when he was introduced to Compeyson, a forger and swindler, who managed to get him and keep him in his debt in order to make him do his dirty work for him. Two or three years later (he refers in passing to this in Ch.42 and Herbert tells Pip more details he has had from Magwitch in Ch.50) he become involved with a feisty and violently jealous young woman. She was about 20 years old and Magwitch was now 35. They he had a daughter, born in 1805. Two or three years later this common-law wife was tried for the murder of an older woman who Magwitch seems to have developed some sort of relationship with. She was acquitted, largely due to Jaggers' representation of her, but swore to kill the child as revenge against Magwitch. Pip is able (later) to work out that the child lived, and is in fact Estella, and that the mother is Jaggers' housekeeper Molly: Magwitch, however, believes the child dead and has no idea what became of Molly. Jaggers advises Pip against telling him. Magwitch laid low during the trial for fear that he would have to mention the child and that Molly would be hanged for its murder, but Compeyson used this fear as another means by which to control him. Eventually Magwitch and Compeyson are both tried, Compeyson's lawyer managing to convince the court that the younger man was influenced by the older Magwitch, who had a long criminal record. Compeyson, the man behind the criminal enterprise, gets the lighter sentence and Magwitch swears revenge. When they both end up on the same prison ship, Magwitch tries to attack him and is put in solitary confinement below, from where he escapes. This is when he meets Pip on the marshes. Returning to the events described in Ch.1-5 of the novel, the cold and starving Magwitch is fed and helped by the young Pip, who mentions another escaped convict he has seen, whom Magwitch knows to be Compeyson. Instead of getting away, Magwitch tracks down and attacks Compeyson, but both are recaptured while fighting.

In Ch. 42 Magwitch describes how he was tried again and deported to Australia where he had to serve out his sentence. He could never return to Britain on pain of death.

What happened next is related in Ch.39, when he explains the source of his wealth to Pip. On his release from the penal colony he became a sheep-farmer and stock-breeder and became very rich - but he had sworn to himself that all the money he made was to make Pip a gentleman. He arranged with Jaggers, whom he remembered from Molly's trial, for Pip, at 18, to be anonymously given a generous allowance and given a proper gentleman's education. Five years later he made the journey back to London under the name Provis, and revealed himself to a shocked and ungrateful Pip.

Pip was also fearful for him, however, and planned to get him out of the country where he would be safe. He hides him in a safe house under the name of Mr Campbell. Unfortunately Compeyson is also in London and learns of Magwitch's return. He knows that Magwitch will attack him if he discovers him and arranges with the authorities for Magwitch to be arrested when he breaks cover to escape down the Thames. Seeing Compeyson on the boat sent out to arrest him, Magwitch launches himself at Compeyson and they both go under. Compeyson is drowned, and the mortally injured Magwitch is arrested. Pip visits him every day in Newgate prison then in hospital until he dies of his injuries, not before being sentenced to death for returning to England. As he is dying, Pip tells him that his daughter is alive, very beautiful, and that he, Pip, loves her.

Character:

Magwitch is an essentially good-hearted man to whom a lot of bad things have happened and who, in turn, has done a lot of bad things. The wrong things he does are, however, largely about survival, not about self-enrichment. His gratitude to Pip and the steadfastness with which he is determined to give Pip a helping hand seems to motivate his success as a sheep-farmer, and he never wavers in his resolve that Pip, not he, should be the beneficiary: he lives frugally while he accumulates wealth. Even when cold and hungry on the marshes at the start of the story- though he uses threats to get Pip to do his bidding- he softens when Pip returns. Just as he is steadfast in holding to the promise he made to himself to make Pip a gentleman, however, he is steadfast in his desire for revenge on Compeyson. This determined single-mindedness, which has made it possible for him to survive and thrive, has the downside, however of blinding him to Pip's unease about taking the money he has made. Unsurprisingly, given his life, sensitivity to nuance and the wishes of others is not his strong point. He dies content, unaware that Pip will lose all the money he made for him, comforted (we assume) by the news that his beautiful daughter has won Pip's heart.

ESTELLA

Biography:

Estella did not have a good start in life. She was the illegitimate daughter of at 37-year vagrant with a long criminal record, working for a fraudster, and a violently jealous and vengeful 22-year old wild woman. When she is two or three years old, her mother is tried for the murder of another woman that she suspects the father of having an affair with. Though she is found not guilty, largely due to the cleverness of the lawyer Jaggers, her vengeance is still not satisfied, and she threatens to kill her daughter (it's not clear what name she went by at this stage) to further hurt the father. Jaggers takes the woman, Molly, as his housekeeper and the father (Magwitch) is soon jailed and then deported. Neither sees the daughter again.

Estella's luck seems to change when she is adopted- through Jaggers- by a wealthy heiress, Miss Havisham. Miss Havisham is 36 years old and unmarried and later claimed to Pip that she sincerely wanted a girl child to care for. It is Miss Havisham that names her Estella - we are not told what her name had been previously. However it is not a healthy environment for the young child. Miss Havisham is still traumatised by having been jilted on her wedding day ten years earlier. She closed the curtains and stopped the clocks at that time and has allowed nothing to change in Satis House, the mansion in which she lives. She has not left the house or seen daylight in all that time, and never again will. She keeps a minimal staff and is visited, it appears, only by her relatives interested in inheriting some of her wealth and Jaggers, who looks after her business and legal matters for her. Pumblechook visits to pay rent, as presumably do other tenants, but he has never actually seen her. Although Estella is not similarly confined, and is free to roam the grounds, this is not a healthy environment in which to grow up.

When Mss Havisham sees that Estella is an exceptionally attractive child, she determined that she would never get hurt in the way that she herself had, by teaching her to be insulated from feeling. But over time this wrong-headed attempt at doing the right thing became further warped into fashioning Estella into somebody who could exact revenge on all men for the hurt Miss Havisham had suffered at the hands on one man.

When eight-year-old Pip is first sent to Satis House as a playmate for her, Estella, also eight years old, is a pretty, but spoilt child whose sense of superiority to Pip is encouraged by Miss Havisham. She enjoys Pip's increasing infatuation with her, but uses it to humiliate him. It is noteworthy that the only time that she seems to respond favourably to Pip is when he soundly beats the young Herbert, son of Miss Havisham's cousin Matthew, in a boxing match that she secretly watches.

Sometime around the age of fifteen or sixteen, Estella is sent abroad by Miss Havisham as a form of 'finishing' and does not return, apparently, until Ch.27, when she is eighteen or nineteen. When Pip is called to Satis House in Ch. 29 Estella is present. Now grown up, she is more refined and well-mannered and more aware of the damage done to her: she knows she is incapable of love, but cares enough about Pip to try to warn him of this.

She is sent to stay with Mrs Brandley, and old friend of Miss Havisham in Richmond - not yet engulfed by London at that time. From there she enjoys a freer social life and is much sort after by young men, though still playing them along skilfully as she has been trained to do. By Ch.38 she is beginning to free herself of Miss Havisham's absolute control over her and on a visit to Satis House they argue for the first time in Pip's presence.

As mentioned, Estella might be unable to feel love, but she is not, as an adult, uncaring: she repeatedly tries to warn Pip off hoping for her love and treats him with respect, not as one of the suitors she toys with.

> "Do you want me then", said Estella, turning suddenly with a fixed and serious, if not angry, look, "to deceive and entrap you?"
> "Do you deceive and entrap him, Estella?"
> "Yes, and many others—all of them but you."

This is not, of course, what Pip wants, but she is actually doing him a kindness. When she marries the boorish Bentley Drummle, it is, she admits, partly because he is too insensitive to feel the lack of love in her. It is also possible that she knows, perhaps subconsciously, that his level brutishness might be what she needs in order to feel something. It is perhaps relevant to remember here how she responded to watching the young Pip bloodying the young Herbert - the pale young gentleman - the only time, as a child, that she showed Pip anything other than disdain.

When Pip meets her again, in the final chapter of the book, eleven or twelve years after the main story, Drummle is dead and she tells Pip that:

"...suffering has been stronger than all other teaching, and has taught me to understand what your heart used to be. I have been bent and broken, but -- I hope -- into a better shape."

She is older and wiser, and the deliberately ambiguous end holds out hope that Pip and she will finally be united. This was not, of course, the end Dickens originally wrote - in that she was married again, but to a better, kinder man, and Pip was able to be free of his longing for her because, in a way, it was the hurt in her that made him unable either to have her or let go of her.

Character:

Estella's character is so manipulated by Miss Havisham that it's difficult to get at what she's actually like underneath. It's clear that she has some of her mother's fieriness which breaks surface from time to time in rebelliousness or attraction of the more brutal and less refined side of men. She is also intelligent - she easily beats Pip at card games and is later able to hold her own in educated society. As an adult, towards those whose passions are strong enough to break through the callous and heartless persona she has been trained into. She is, in fact, a caring person. She is fully aware of the damage done to her, but unable to undo it - though she maybe instinctively knows that she needs to suffer to do this. This suffering comes full circle - Miss Havisham closed down due to the cruelty of a man and trained Estella to be closed to feeling: Estella needed to suffer cruelty from another man to open herself to feeling.

Miss HAVISHAM

Biography:

Miss Havisham's back story is related in outline by Herbert, the son of her cousin Matthew Pocket, in Ch.22, although other bits are revealed along the way.

Working back from Dickens' note that she was 56 at the start of Part III of the novel, she would have been born in about 1772. Her mother died when she was a baby, leaving her an only child, but her father, a wealthy country gentleman and brewer, spoiled her terribly. The mansion in which they lived - Satis House - had the brewery attached, though it had fallen into disrepair by the time the novel is set.

Her father was married again in secret to, Herbert believes, his cook. She bore him a son, but she also died and the son was brought to live with the father and daughter -the first she knew of her father's second marriage. This half-brother, Arthur," *turned out riotous, extravagant, undutiful - altogether bad"* and was disinherited by the father, though given a generous allowance, which he squandered. Arthur held this against Miss Havisham, now heir to the estate (which he, as a son, though younger than she, would have inherited), believing that she had influenced their father's decision. The father died when she was in her mid-twenties and Arthur was 'a young man' - probably about 21. He teamed up with Compeyson, a handsome gentlemanly fraudster of about 22-3 and they set about defrauding Miss Havisham of large sums of money. She was taken in by the deception, falling in love with Compeyson, as he intended, and believing that he meant to marry her. Only Matthew Pocket warned her about Compeyson, and was cut off by her for his efforts. The wedding was arranged, but at twenty to nine on that day she received a letter from Compeyson saying it was off. It's not explained why he didn't marry her and so get his hands on all her wealth, but Herbert speculates that he might have already been married or that this was part of Arthur's cruel revenge.

Miss Havisham has a mental breakdown as a result of this trauma and tries to stop time: she stops the clocks at twenty to nine and closes the curtains so she will never see another day. The food on the wedding table, including the cake, is left to rot, and the part of the house to slowly fall into disrepair: the brewery, which she was tricked into buying off Arthur, who was given it, falls into total disrepair. She keeps a small staff to attend to basic needs, but we know nothing of her for the next ten years.

At 36 we know that she has taken on Jaggers to manage her financial and legal affairs for her. She is still living as before but is engaging with the world outside her gloomy house more. She has decided that she wants to adopt a daughter to give love to. Jaggers brings her the 2-3year old daughter of a low-life client who is not fit to look after her, having threatened to kill her as revenge on the father. She names the child Estella and commences to bring her up as a lady. When the child is seven, she looks for child as a playmate for Estella and Pumblechook, sensing advantage for himself, suggests the young brother of his nephew Joe's wife, who has been taken on by Joe as a son. This child, also seven years old, is, of course, Pip.

It's clear from the beginning that Miss Havisham (now 40) enjoys seeing Estella humiliate Pip, and indeed connives at it by passing on things Pip believed he had said in confidence. Through several years of Pip's weekly or otherwise visits, as Estella becomes more beautiful and Pip becomes more fixated on her, Miss Havisham seems to realise the potential for using Estella to revenge herself on men for the trauma she suffered.

When Pip and Estella are about 14, and Miss Havisham is 47, she pays for Pip to be apprenticed to Joe as a blacksmith and sends Estella off to Europe to complete her education. However, when Pip's dream of becoming a gentleman is unexpectedly made possible four years later and he naturally assumes that she is behind this, she does nothing to correct his mistake.

When Pip is set up in London, at age 18, Miss Havisham (aged 51) calls him back to Kent to meet up again with Estella. Alone with Pip, she tells him to love Estella no matter how badly she treats him - there is something about the way she does this, described as like a curse, which even Pip, who is unlikely to need this prompting, finds disturbing. He also sees how she manipulates her cousins, especially Sarah Pocket, now living at Satis House, using their greed for her money against them.

Ch.38 sees Estella loosening Miss Havisham's manipulative grip on her, and they argue, leaving Miss Havisham emotionally strained.

Miss Havisham next appears in Ch.24 when Pip (now 23 - she is 56) visits her to say goodbye before, he imagines, leaving England with Magwitch. Pip hurls all his pent up disappointment and unhappiness at finding out that Magwitch is his patron and that she allowed him to believe it was her, and that he therefore believed Estella was for him. When he leaves, having bitterly told Estella how he has always loved her and how he cannot bear that she is marrying Drummle, Miss Havisham, for the first time, appears wracked with pity and remorse.

In Ch. 49, Pip returns to Satis House and asks Miss Havisham if she will complete the funding he has secretly been undertaking of Herbert's business partnership. She is lonely and distracted and authorises the money - a considerable sum - without argument. She has clearly been brooding on their last encounter, and realises how destructive a part she has played in Pip's life. She asks for forgiveness, repeating again and again *'What have I done?'* despite Pip's readiness to give her that forgiveness. As Pip is about to leave, her wedding dress, which she has worn for thirty years, catches fire from the open hearth where she is sitting. Although Pip rushes to her aid, she is badly burned. The doctor thinks that the injuries are not life-threatening, but she never recovers and dies several weeks later while Pip is recovering from his own nervous collapse.

Character:

Dickens' serious characters, however strange, are always plausible, and you can often see him working on this in the back-stories he invents to explain their odd behaviour. This is particularly interesting where the characters, or things that happen to them, are based on real people, as seems to have been the case with Miss Havisham, who is believed to be an amalgam of three ladies, one an Australian recluse. Dickens is fascinated by the strangeness, but also needs to explain it.

Like the other three important characters given detailed descriptions here, she never knew her mother. She also had a step-mother whom she never knew, in that role at least. As the only child of a wealthy man she was spoiled, but this comfortable situation was disrupted by the sudden arrival of a half-brother of whom she knew nothing. She might well have resented his presence, and the fact that this intruder stood to inherit what she must have thought was going to be hers. Whether or not she played a part in her father disinheriting Arthur, her half-brother, she had probably not, as a girl, been trained in the running of the business - so when her father died she was rich and vulnerable - an easy target for a smooth con-man like Compeyson (especially when helped by Arthur). The extent of the trauma she suffered is extreme but, for somebody who grew up as a spoiled child- used to having its own way and protected by an indulgent father- into a woman in her mid-twenties who had never known a mother, had just lost her father, and had probably never been in love before, it is not implausible. Her tragedy is that all her wealth became a curse to her, allowing her to indulge her grievances long past the undoubted breakdown she suffered and to go on nursing her grievances rather than making a life for herself. This was unfortunately only made worse by the fact that the girl child she adopted out of a need to love somebody, turned out beautiful and allowed her thwarted love to turn to revenge against men. It is perhaps significant, though, that she chose an innocent village boy (Pip) as a playmate for the girl (Estella): in doing so she exposed herself to a simple moral goodness (in Pip, though a conflicted character, and strongly, though less often, in Joe) that had *not* been part of her life before. Pip needs to go through his own growing-up moral crises before he has the strength to stand up for what's right and true, but when he does, and when she sees that far from protecting Estella from what she herself suffered, she has cursed her and Pip's love for her, things that have stagnated for thirty years in her start to move: there moments of kindness and wanting to put things right mixed into the habitual self-pity. It is symbolically significant that the wedding dress she has worn for thirty years then catches fire, but it's also her tragedy that the healing she needs can never take place because of this final trauma. She was able to make some form of amends to Matthew and Herbert Pocket, but not able to accept forgiveness from Pip and move on.

Dickens had strong moral intent in his writing and Miss Havisham can perhaps be seen as personifying the dangers of being unable to forgive or accept forgiveness.

PIP

Biography:

Great Expectations is essentially the fictional Pip's account of a significant and formative time in his life, from the age of seven to the age of about twenty-four, with a brief last chapter featuring events about eleven years later - the time, one supposes, that the story was written. The story is thus written from the perspective of somebody who has lived through the events, knows their outcome and has had time to gain a little perspective on them.

Pip was born in 1805 and orphaned shortly afterwards. What happened to his parents is never explained though his sister, his only surviving relative, and her husband, Joe must have known. Between his sister, Georgiana (named after their mother) and himself, Philip Pirrip (named after their father) there were five brothers who died in infancy (thus the rest of the family didn't all die in one tragic event). He is known as Pip, as this is the way he pronounces his own name as a young child.

Pip grows up close to where he was born (and his parents and brothers are buried) on the North Kent marshes. When his parents died he has 'cared for' by his somewhat shrewish and resentful sister, twenty years his senior, and taken on by the kindly village blacksmith, Joe, when she marries him.

Pip is seven years old and living at the forge when the story starts, on Christmas Eve (1812).

He is visiting the graves of parents when surprised by an escaped convict who threatens him and tells him to bring him food and a file to remove his manacles. The frightened Pip steals food from home (more and better food than strictly necessary) and a file from the forge and takes them to the convict, who is soon caught; but Pip, who is there when it happens, is able to signal that he didn't tell the authorities anything. At home he is bullied and belittled by his sister and Joe's Uncle Pumblechook along with various other neighbours, but has a friend in Joe.

During the course of the following year, Pumblechook, looking to find favour with the eccentric Miss Havisham, the wealthy landlady of his business premises, suggests Pip as a playmate for her young adopted daughter, Estella. Thus starts a relationship that will change Pip's life. Estella is proud and rude, but Pip is drawn to her and his discontent with the future mapped out for him as an apprentice blacksmith- eventually taking over Joe's business- starts.

When he begins his (very inadequate) schooling he meets Biddy, another orphan, but a year older than him and a very quick learner, who becomes a life-long friend. She helps with his education.

More or less frequent visits to Miss Havisham continue until Pip reaches the age of 14. Miss Havisham calls Joe in and pays for Pip's apprenticeship. Pip, who is becoming smitten with the increasingly beautiful Estella- and more than ever sure that he wants to be a gentleman, not a blacksmith- is devastated, but equally doesn't want to hurt Joe, who has shown him nothing but kindness.

Four years later the London lawyer Jaggers, who manages Miss Havisham's affairs, informs the eighteen-year-old Pip that he has Great Expectations. He is to be released from his apprenticeship and taken to live in London (some thirty miles away) where he will receive a generous allowance and be educated as a gentleman. At an unspecified time his benefactor will make themselves known to him and he will come into a substantial fortune. The only conditions are that he is always known as Pip, and that he never tries to find out the identity of his benefactor. These circumstances conspire to make Pip sure that it is Miss Havisham who is behind it and he becomes increasingly certain that her motive is to make him a suitable husband for Estella. This connection is further strengthened as Pip is to be tutored by Matthew Pocket, Miss Havisham's cousin, and shares lodgings with his son, Herbert.

At Matthew Pocket's house, Pip meets two other students, the stupid and boorish Bentley Drummle and the much more pleasant Startop. He makes friends with Jaggers' clerk Wemmick, who is a valuable source of help and advice. Although getting a good allowance, Pip lives beyond his means and his life becomes a bit lacking in purpose. During this period he continues to distance himself from his past while knowing how ungrateful he is being. It is during this period that his sister, Joe's wife, finally dies from injuries received in an attack some years earlier. Pip returns for her funeral and sleeps at the forge, but is out of place and argues unfairly with Biddy, who has become Joe's housekeeper.

When Estella returns from a number of years in Europe more beautiful and graceful than eve, Pip's infatuation with her is re-ignited, and he is sure that they are meant for one another, deafening himself to her warnings that she is incapable of love. He tortures himself with attending on her in Richmond while she toys with suitors - particularly, and increasingly, Bentley Drummle. Meanwhile, Pip has decided to try to do some good with his money and started the process of buying the impoverished Herbert into a partnership in a trading company.

Pip's twenty-first birthday comes and goes and he still hasn't come into his 'expectations'. At the end of Part 2 he is about to go to bed in his and Herbert's new Temple lodgings when a stranger, whom he soon discovers to be the convict he met at the start of the story, reveals himself as Pip's benefactor.

The convict, Abel Magwitch, after having been deported and doing well for himself in Australia, has returned illegally to England to see the gentleman he has made. Pip is thrown into confusion and horrified, not just that such an un-gentlemanly person should be the source of his expectations but at the realisation that if it isn't Miss Havisham, then Estella is not intended for him.

Pip decides that he must get Magwitch out of the country for his own safety (the penalty for returning to England is death), and that he cannot take any more of Magwitch's money, however much Magwitch has dreamed of his having it. Meanwhile, Magwitch must be put in a safe house and kept away from Pip as Pip might be a known contact who could be followed.

Pip realises that if he doesn't take the money then he can't afford to continue paying for Herbert's business partnership, so he goes to see Miss Havisham to ask her to help her relative. Estella is also there, and Pip tells her of his love, but she says she is to marry Drummle. He is distraught - not just at her marrying somebody else, but at that person being Drummle.

Sometime later, Pip returns to Miss Havisham formerly asking her for the money for Herbert. Finding her wracked with despair about the harm she has done, he willingly forgives her any hurt she might have done him. As he is leaving, her dress catches fire and, though he saves her life, he receives painful burns himself. In the meantime, he has been putting together scraps of information that lead him to realise that Estella is the daughter of Magwitch and Jaggers' maid Molly, but accepts Jaggers' warning that no good can come of telling any of them.

Just before he is going to row Magwitch down the Thames to catch a boat bound for Europe, he is tricked into returning to an isolated place on the marshes where Orlick, a jobbing workman who worked for Joe, says he is going to kill him for interfering with his unwanted attentions to Biddy and losing him a job as gatekeeper for Miss Havisham. Orlick also admits to having attacked his sister. Pip is saved by Herbert and others.

The next day, however, when they try to escape with Magwitch, they are intercepted by the authorities and Magwitch, badly injured in the process, is taken to jail where he dies before he can be hanged for returning. Pip stays with him during his last days, not telling him that all his money is forfeit to the crown - allowing him to believe that Pip will live well on it as he intended - but telling him right at the end of his life that his daughter (Estella) is alive and very beautiful and that he, Pip, loves her.

Pip then suffers a form of nervous collapse and is nursed back to health by Joe. He determines that all along Biddy was the girl for him, but when he returns to his village, she is already married to Joe. Pip goes off to join Herbert who is running the Cairo branch of the business Pip secretly bought him into.

The final chapter is set eleven years after the main story. Pip has worked his way up to being a partner in the business and comes back to visit Joe and Biddy and their son, Pip, for the first time. Looking over the demolished ruins of Miss Havisham's house, he meets Estella, who had a terrible marriage; Drummle is now dead. As narrator, Pip makes it clear that Estella, now more able to feel love, asks for friendship, but he still wants love, and has no reason to doubt that they will finally be united.

Character:

In many ways the Pip we watch growing up through the story isn't a very likeable person - but he is redeemed by two things: first, that the book is supposedly written by an older Pip looking back, and he is, if anything, more appalled by some of his behaviour than we are, and second, we might ask ourselves how differently we would behave in the same circumstances.

Pip never knew his parents, his sister seems to have only reluctantly looked after him until she married Joe Gargery, who was a kind and decent man, but was easily intimidated by his wife and by his social 'superiors'. Pip's sister, Mrs Joe, along with Pumblechook and others, constantly tells the young Pip how grateful he should be that she has taken him on and brought him up 'by hand'. Pip is essentially honest, but quickly to compromise where his honesty is punished. He is introduced by

Pumblechook to Miss Havisham out of Pumblechook's wish to gain favour with his wealthy landlady, not for Pip's own good, and is made to feel miserable, clumsy and inadequate by the treatment he receives from her and Estella. (Nobody other than Jaggers knew at this stage quite how un-genteel Estella's own background was, though Miss Havisham would have known she was an unwanted child.)

Miss Havisham then summarily cuts off her relationship with Pip, giving him over to Joe to be apprenticed. He is granted an annual visit on his birthday, but now has to knuckle down to a future as village blacksmith, having tasted the life of a gentleman, and wanting it for himself - not least so that he stands a chance with Estella, with whom he has become infatuated.

This conflict in himself really comes into play when, out of the blue, he is lifted out of his circumstances, and given the chance to be a gentleman. To be fair to Pip, we all need to break free from our backgrounds before we can be fully adult, but he is very aware of his ingratitude to Joe (who released him, wanting only what was best for him) but only agonises over it, not puts things right. He is blinded by his infatuation for Estella into seeing everything in terms of their relationship, and won't hear her warnings that she is incapable of love.

In his defence, that is a very human reaction, and he is somebody who has never had a strong father figure (Joe, although he stubbornly knows right from wrong and will make a stand on such issues, has a very small comfort zone and treats Pip as a friend, not as a son), but know only a succession of people who tried to shape him to meet their own requirements or wishes. Even Matthew Pocket, though, like Joe, a decent man with moral courage, is also a little ineffectual, as is his son, Herbert.

Pip takes a big step forward when he decides to help Herbert anonymously, and a bigger one when he confronts Miss Havisham with what she has done to Estella and himself. He takes an even bigger one when he willingly forgives her for this. This is important as he is slowly releasing himself from the power she has over him.

Pip's relationship with Magwitch is also problematic, but ultimately the making of Pip. Pip's disappointment that it is not Miss Havisham who is his benefactor - based on the belief he'd allowed himself to entertain that this meant that Estella was intended for him - makes him enormously ungrateful for the gift that he has benefited happily from -and blind to the irony that his revulsion to the person of Magwitch is as a result of the change in himself brought about by Magwitch's money. However, when he decides he wants none of Magwitch's money, though in itself a slight to the person who has endured much hardship on his behalf (however much Pip might claim he never asked him to), he takes an important step towards growing up. Released of this obligation, he starts to treat Magwitch with increasing sympathy and ends up caring for him. This sets him on the path that ultimately allows him to be part of a business of which he could say: *We were not in a grand way of business, but we had a good name, and worked for our profits, and did very well.*

Despite believing the contrary several times, Pip never frees himself from Estella. He never marries, or even, as far as we know, has a serious relationship with any other woman, and when he meets her by chance at the end of the story, his wish is still to be with her.

However, as mentioned, it has to be remembered that the story is (fictionally) written by Pip. That he so clearly sees his earlier failings, makes it clear that he has grown up and put them mostly behind him. He is a person who is happy to be part of a well-respected and hard-working company, and one senses he has found his place in the world at last - his own place, not one foisted on him by others.

Character	Age	Significance
Bentley Drummle	Drummle is about a year older than Pip, so he is about **19** when we first meet him. He married Estella in his **mid-20s** and dies in his **mid-30s**.	Interestingly in contrast to Pip, and Pip's ambitions, Bentley Drummle is a gentleman by birth - 'the next heir but one to a baronetcy' (Ch.23) - but anything but a gentleman by manners. Our picture of him is coloured by (the narrator) Pip's intense dislike of him, but this frequently appears justified. Described at the start of Ch.25, he is boorish and stupid although Jaggers takes an unaccountable liking to him (even though calling him the Spider, suggesting - perceptively - that he will wait patiently but unwaveringly to get what he wants). Pip, the (fictitious) narrator is looking back on his life from a time significantly after the events described, and so his animus towards Drummle is heightened by the fact that Drummle goes on to marry Estella, whom Pip has been in love with since he was a child. In his marriage Drummle is 'notoriously cruel' and brutal while squandering Estella's inheritance from Miss Havisham. The couple separate while Pip is overseas and Drummle dies as a result of his mistreatment of a horse.
Biddy	Biddy is a year older than Pip, so **8-9** when we first meet her and about **25** when she marries Joe	Biddy is the orphaned granddaughter of Mr. Wopsle's great aunt who runs the wholly inadequate evening school (and shop) in Pip's village where Biddy and Pip first meet as children. As a child she is not well cared for, but very quick at learning and, being a year or two older than Pip and of a very giving nature, is responsible for a lot of Pip's early education. When her grandmother dies a little while after Mrs Joe is attacked, she becomes Joe's live-in housekeeper at about the age of sixteen. She is quite ordinary looking and Pip, dazzled by Estella's beauty, is blind to the fact that she is attracted to him as a teenager, though valuing her friendship and advice (even if the latter is not always what he wants to hear). When Joe's wife dies, she has to move out of his house, and becomes a school-mistress at a new village school. She continues to spend time with Joe, however, teaching him to read and write and no doubt doing some housekeeping for him while Pip is away in London. She ends up marrying Joe who, although twenty years older than her, is well matched in terms of essential goodness and moral strength. Pip, after losing his expectations, finally comes to value her (and Joe) uncritically for this.
Compeyson	In Dickens' notes Compeyson is **52-3** at the time of his death. Makes him about **22-3** when he jilted Miss Havisham and in his **mid-30s**	Compeyson doesn't appear in person except right at the beginning and right at the end of the story, but has a major influence on the events that shape Pip's life. He is clever and charming and from a good background, but makes his money by fraud, his most successful being against Miss Havisham an league with her half-brother Arthur. It was this that caused her to shut out the world and train Estella to be heartless in revenge against men - both of which profoundly affect Pip. He also once employed Magwitch in his criminal activities, which led to Magwitch's trial and deportation while he got off lightly. This created a feud between them which led to Compeyson's betraying of Magwitch to the authorities on his illegal return to

	when Pip first sees him on the marsh	England, resulting in both of their deaths and the loss of Pip's 'expectations'. Compeyson is also involved in Orlick's attempt to kill Pip. Thus Compeyson is indirectly responsible for all the events that take Pip from being a village boy destined to be a blacksmith to the person he ends up as - but only through the intervention of the good people Pip meets along the way and Pip's own moral courage at important moments does it turn out well for Pip.
Herbert	Herbert is about Pip age being about **7** when we meet him in Ch. 11, **18-23** in part II and **23-24** in part III.	Herbert is first encountered as the pale young gentleman of about Pip's age who challenged the young Pip to a fight during a visit to Satis house. Pip notes that he has a blindly optimistic view of his own performance, a characteristic that stays with him to some extent later in his search for employment - though at the end of the novel Pip wonders if he has always been more competent that he appears. Herbert is the eldest son of Matthew Pocket, a cousin of Miss Havisham and a gentleman by birth, though not by fortune. Jaggers recommends Matthew as a tutor for Pip in London, and Herbert and Pip are thrown together sharing an apartment first at Barnard's Inn, later at Temple. He proves a loyal and largely uncritical friend to Pip who Pip secretly secures a future for when he has money, and who gives Pip a home when he loses it.
Jaggers	Dickens' notes say Jaggers is **55** in part III, so he will have been about **40** when Pip first sees him at Satis house, and 50 when he in introduced as Pip's guardian. He is in about **35** at the time of Molly's trial	Jaggers the attorney is an enigmatic character, but one whose position and influence are crucial in putting the pieces in place that will determine the course of Pip's life. It is he who defended Molly (Estella's mother and Magwitch's 'wife') and through whom an otherwise implausible set of co-incidences make sense. He is a very clever and careful man, but one who keeps others at a distance. He is essentially a moral man who believes deeply in justice, though he presents himself as cynically pragmatic. He is also very charismatic, though not very prepossessing in appearance, and his clerks and clients are in awe of him - notably the clerk Wemmick, who adopts a totally different persona when at work to his home self. Yet he has strange quirks - like his habit of biting his finger, his taking a shine to Bentley Drummle and his almost compulsive hand-washing in a way that seems symbolic of not wanting to be tainted by the world he inhabits. He appears to live alone (in Gerrard Street, Soho) with Molly as his housekeeper.
Joe	Joe is **45** in part three, which makes him about **29** at the start of the story and about **57** in chapter fifty-nine	Joe Gargery is the village blacksmith in Pip's village and nephew to Mr Pumblechook. Though an intelligent and capable man he had a difficult childhood with a domineering alcoholic father who would not let his caring mother send him to school. He is married to Pip's older sister, Georgiana, known as Mrs Joe. He also takes on caring for the orphaned Pip from a young age. Quite why this strong but gentle man should have married, and been dominated by, the shrewish Georgiana is not fully explained, but he does describe her as 'a fine figure of a woman' (though the marriage remains childless). Pip suspects that Mrs Joe made Joe marry her 'by hand', but Joe implies in chapter 7

		that, along with some sort of attraction, there was a level of sympathy for both her and Pip (who she already looking after) in his decision. This is certainly the case later when Joe takes the orphan Biddy as a housekeeper when her grandmother dies. Joe remains good-hearted and forgiving even to his father and even when Pip is clearly embarrassed by his social awkwardness away from his own home and people and avoids seeing him. Joe's essential goodness does however make a lasting mark on Pip, although in some ways it also drives the ambitious young Pip away from his village as he feels constantly rebuked by it, and it is Joe who nurses Pip through his illness in part three. He married Biddy after Mrs Joe dies, and they call their son Pip.
Mr Pumblechook	Pumblechook is Joe's uncle, and while no age is given, it would be reasonable to assume that this makes him in the region of 20 years older than Joe	Pumblechook is a classic Dickens hypocrite - in this case a man who always makes out that he is acting for others while pursuing self-interest - who delights in putting Pip down as a child, the moment Pip's fortunes change, he tries to ingratiate himself with Pip, and puts it about that he is responsible for Pip's elevation. Here he makes the same mistake as Pip himself does in assuming that Miss Havisham is the source of Pip's great expectations - Pumblechook having been responsible for putting Pip forward when he became aware that Miss Havisham was looking for a playmate for her ward, Estella. He likewise attributes Pip's loss of fortune to his ingratitude towards him. He is in fact Joe's uncle, but it through the more like-minded Mrs Joe that he is welcomed into the family and allowed to exert influence.
Mrs. Joe	Mrs Joe is **20** years older than Pip She is in her **early 30s** when attacked by Orlick and dies at about **39**	Georgina Maria Gargery (née Pirrip) is Pip's only known surviving blood relative. Her parents died shortly after Pip's birth, but we are not told how. She is Pip's oldest sibling, called after her mother, and there were five other brothers between them who died in infancy. She took over bringing Pip up, but did not seem to be doing a very good job, as he was very small for his age when she married Joe. She is not an appealing character as seen through the eyes of Pip the narrator. She is bad-tempered and domineering - not just with Pip but with Joe as well. We are left to assume that she married Joe out of desperation rather than affection, though he regarded her as a 'fine figure of a woman.' She has a stick - 'Tickler' - with which she regularly beats Pip -and Joe! She also constantly reminds Pip how she has brought him up 'by hand', and that he should be grateful. She collects friends, including Uncle Pumblechook, who is actually Joe's uncle, who share her views. She plays on Joe's weaknesses by constantly wearing a dirty apron, suggesting that she is a domestic slave like his mother, and, like his father, disapproves of him being educated. After a revenge attack by Orlick, which appears to result in some brain damage, she becomes better natured but severely disabled. She eventually dies of her injuries, showing in her last moments some affection for Joe.
Orlick	Orlick is **25** mid-way through Pt.	Dolge Orlick is a journeyman labourer who appears somewhat out of the blue in Ch.15 (when Pip is about 13) though he has worked for Joe since Pip was a small child. He is described as

	1, making him about **30** at the start of Pt. 2 and **35** in Pt. 3 (and about **47** in Ch. 59.)	slouching and surly in manner and is very vengeful by nature. He attacks Mrs Joe, leaving her for dead after she demands that Joe fight him for insulting her. He carries a more understandable grudge against Pip (who was favoured over him as an apprentice to Joe, came between him and his rather fanciful hopes of marrying Biddy, and lost him his job with Miss Havisham) to the extreme of luring him out onto the marshes to attempt to kill him. To some extent his grievances against Pip are justified - though his means of redressing them are not - and it is largely due to Pip's and Mrs Joe's interventions that he goes from being a useful worker with an attitude problem to a violent criminal locked up in jail. Perhaps this is to see things with a 21st century perspective though - in the 19th century his fate would have been regarded as the result only of his bad character to all but the most subtle minds. such as Dickens'.
Wemmick		Described at the beginning of Ch.21, John Wemmick is one of the few endearing characters in Great Expectations. He is a clerk in Jaggers' office, very much Jaggers' right-hand-man, where his persona is dry and wooden - but when he leaves work he gradually relaxes into another self, which is warm and playful - and a good friend to Pip. Perhaps his most endearing aspect is the wooden Castle - complete with moat, drawbridge and canon - he has built as a home for himself and his clearly much loved father, the Aged Parent. It is from this Walworth home that he is married, in part 3, to Miss Skiffins, a relationship that is useful to Pip as it is through her brother that he finds employment for Herbert.

Name	aka	who/what	first mention
Abel Magwitch	*see* Magwitch		
Abraham (Pirrip)		name on grave - older brother of Pip, died in infancy/childhood	Ch. 1
Aged Parent	Aged, Aged P.	John Wemmick's father	Ch.25
Alexander (Pirrip)		name on grave - older brother of Pip, died in infancy/childhood	Ch. 1
Alick (Pocket)		young son of Matthew Pocket	Ch.22
Amelia	'Melia	client of Jaggers	Ch.20
Arthur Havisham	Arthur	Miss Havisham's half-brother, con-man colleague of Compeyson	Ch.42
Avenger (the)	Pepper	Pip's servant boy in	Ch.27
Baby		youngest of Matthew Pocket's children	Ch23
Barley, Mr	Bill Barley, Old Barley, Gruffandgrim	Clara's father	Ch.46
Bartholomew (Pirrip)		name on grave - older brother of Pip, died in infancy/childhood	Ch. 1
Belinda	*see* Mrs. Pocket		
Bentley Drummle	Spider, Drummle	*See main characters*	Ch.23
Biddy		*See main characters*	Ch.7
Bill		client of Jaggers	Ch.20
Bill Barley	*see* Mr, Barley	Clara's father	Ch.46
Black Bill		Newgate prisoner	Ch.32
Boots		presumably junior staffer at Blue Boar	Ch.28
Bounceable		one of the plaster casts of executed criminals in Jaggers' office	Ch.24
Brandley, Mrs		Estella's Richmond landlady, a friend of Miss Havisham from before her seclusion	Ch.38
Briton		Wemmick's refers to the butcher he bought meat for Pips first meal with him as old Briton	Ch.25
Camilla		Matthew Pocket's sister, cousin to Miss Havisham	Ch. 11
Camilla, Mr	*see* Raymond		
Campbell, Mr	*see* Magwitch	name used by Magwitch when in hiding at Mrs Whimple's - *see main characters*	Ch.46
Captain Tom		Newgate prisoner	Ch.32

Charlotte (Pocket)		Herbert's sister who died at fourteen	Ch.30
Clara (Barley)		Herbert's wife to be/ wife	Ch.30
Clarriker		Young merchant who takes Herbert on.	Ch.37
Coiler, Mrs		tediously flattering neighbour to Pockets	Ch.23
Colonel		Newgate prisoner	Ch.32
Compeyson		*See main characters*	(Ch.3) Ch.42
Dolge Orlick	*see* Orlick	*See main characters*	Ch.15
Drummle	*see* Bentley Drummle or Estella	*See main characters*	
Dunstable		local butcher referred to by Pumblechook	Ch.4
Estella	Mrs Bentley Drummle	*See main characters*	Ch.8
Fanny (Pocket)		Matthew's young daughter - Fanny was a popular pet form of Frances	Ch.22
Finches of the Grove		Expensive eating and quarrelling club joined by Pip and Herbert	Ch.34
Flopson		nurse to Matthew Pocket's children	Ch.22
Georgiana		cousin of Miss Havisham	Ch.11
Georgiana (Pirrip)		Pip's deceased mother	Ch.1
Georgiana Maria	*see* Mrs. Joe		
Gruffandgrim	Mr. Barley, Bill Barley	Herbert's nickname for Bill Barley, Clara's father	Ch.46
Habraham Latharuth (Abraham Lazarus)		client of Jaggers	Ch.20
Handel	Pip, Philip Pirrip	Herbert's name for Pip - *see main characters*	Ch.21
Havisham, Miss		*See main characters*	Ch.7
Herbert Pocket	pale young gentleman, Herbert, Pip's comrade (by Magwitch)	*See main characters*	Ch.11 (boy) Ch.21 (man)
Hubble, Mr		wheelwright in Pip's village, part of Mrs Joe's social group	Ch.4
Hubble, Mrs		wife of Mr Hubble, part of Mrs Joe's social group	Ch.4
Jaggers	Mr. Jaggers	*See main characters*	Ch.11
Jane (Pocket)		Matthew's young daughter	Ch.22
Joe (Pocket)		Matthew's young son	Ch.22
Joe Gargery	Joe, Joseph, Mr Gargery	*See main characters*	Ch. 1
John	Wemmick	*See main characters*	

Magwitch	Convict, my convict (Pip), Mr Magwitch, Abel Magwitch, Provis, Mr Campbell	*See main characters*	Ch.1
Mary Anne		Wemmick's servant girl	Ch.45
Matthew Pocket		Cousin to Miss Havisham, husband to Belinda, father to Herbert, tutor to Pip	Ch.11
Mike		client of Jaggers	Ch. 20
Millers		nurse to Matthew Pocket's children	Ch.22
Molly		Estella's mother (by Magwitch), Jaggers' maid	Ch.26
Mrs Joe	Mrs Joe Gargery, Mum, Georgiana M'ria	*See main characters*	Ch.1
Mum		Mrs Joe is called 'Mum' by Pumblechook (not by Pip), and Mrs Pocket by Flopson	
Old Artful		one of the plaster casts of executed criminals in Jaggers' office	
Orlick	Dolge Orlick, Old Orlick, Mr. Orlick	*See main characters*	Ch.15
Pepper	*see* Avenger		
Philip Pirrip (1)		Pip's deceased father	Ch.1
Philip Pirrip (2)	*see* Pip		
Pip	Philip Pirrip, Mr Pip, Handel	*See main characters*	Ch.1
Pip (2)		Joe and Biddy's son	Ch. 59
Pocket, Mrs	Belinda	wife of Matthew Pocket	Ch.22
Potkins	William Potkins	waiter at The Blue Boar, called on by Pumblechook as witness	Ch.58
Provis	*see* Magwitch		
Pumblechook, Mr	Uncle Pumblechook, Pumblechook, Uncle	*See main characters*	Ch.4
Raymond	Cousin Raymond, Mr. Camilla	Camilla's husband	Ch.11
Roger (Pirrip)		name on grave - older brother of Pip, died in infancy/childhood	Ch. 1
Sally		Compeyson's wife	Ch.42
Sarah Pocket		cousin to Miss Havisham	Ch.11

Skiffins		Miss Skiffins' brother - instrumental in obtaining position for Herbert.	Ch.37
Skiffins, Miss		Wemmick's wife to be/ wife	Ch.37
Sophia		housemaid to Pockets	Ch.23
Spider		Jaggers' name for Bentley Drummle - *See main characters*	
Squires		landlord of The Blue Boar	Ch.58
Startop		friend of Pip (student of Matthew Pocket)	Ch.23
Stinger		Wemmick's canon	Ch.24
Tickler		Mrs Joe's cane, used for beating Pip (and Joe)	Ch.2
Tobias (Pirrip)		name on grave - older brother of Pip, died in infancy/childhood	Ch. 1
Tom		Person whose wife's death Matthew wasn't prepared to mourn 'properly'.	Ch.11
Trabb, Mr		Tailor and funeral director in Pip's village	Ch.19
Trabb's boy	Mr Trabb's boy	Mr Trabb's impudent young assistant	Ch.19
Waldengarver, Mr		stage name of Mr Wopsle	Ch. 21
Wemmick	Mr Wemmick, John	*See main characters*	Ch.20
Whimple, Mrs		landlady to Mr, Barley and Clara, hides Magwitch prior to attempted escape	Ch.46
Wopsle , Mr	Mr Waldengarver	clerk at church in Pip's village, later actor in London	Ch.4

Friends and enemies

Name	aka	status	who/what	first mention
Bentley Drummle	Spider	*enemy*	*See main characters*	Ch.23
Biddy		*friend*	*See main characters*	Ch.7
Camilla		enemy	Matthew Pocket's sister, cousin to Miss Havisham	Ch. 11
Clara (Barley)		Change opinion	Herbert's wife to be/ wife	Ch.30
Clarriker		*friend*	Young merchant who takes Herbert on.	Ch.37
Estella		Change opinion	*See main characters*	Ch.8
Georgiana		*enemy*	cousin of Miss Havisham	Ch.11
Havisham, Miss		Change opinion	*See main characters*	Ch.7
Herbert Pocket		*friend*	*See main characters*	Ch.11 (boy) Ch.21 (man)
Jaggers		*friend*	*See main characters*	Ch.11
Joe Gargery		*friend*	*See main characters*	Ch. 1
Magwitch		Change opinion	*See main characters*	Ch.1
Matthew Pocket		*friend*	Cousin to Miss Havisham, husband to Belinda, father to Herbert, tutor to Pip	Ch.11
Mrs Joe		Change opinion	*See main characters*	Ch.1
Orlick	Dolge Orlick,	*enemy*	*See main characters*	Ch.15
Pumblechook, Mr	Uncle	Change with fortune	*See main characters*	Ch.4
Raymond	Mr. Camilla	*enemy*	Camilla's husband	Ch.11
Sarah Pocket		*enemy*	cousin to Miss Havisham	Ch.11
Startop		*friend*	friend of Pip (student of Matthew Pocket)	Ch.23
Trabb, Mr		Change with fortune	Tailor and funeral director in Pip's village	Ch.19
Trabb's boy		*enemy*	Mr Trabb's impudent young assistant	Ch.19
Wemmick	John	*friend*	*See main characters*	Ch.20
Wopsle , Mr	Mr Waldengarver	Change opinion	clerk at church in Pip's village, later actor in London	Ch.4

	CHARACTER AGES										
Year	Pip/Estella/ Herbert	Magwitch	Compeyson	Miss Havisham	Joe	Mrs Joe	Molly	Jaggers	Biddy	Orlick	Event
1768		0									Magwitch born
1772				0							Miss Havisham born
1773								0			Jaggers born
c1776			0								Compeyson born
1783					0		0				Joe & Molly born
1785						0					Mrs Joe born
c1793										0	Orlick born
1798			22-3	26							Comp jilts Miss H
1800		32	24-5	28	17	15	17	27		7(?)	turn of century
c1803									0		Biddy born
1805	0	37	29-30		22	20	22		1-2	12(?)	Pip/E/H born
1808	3	40	32-33	36			25	35			Molly trial/E adopted
1812	7	44	36-7	40	29	27	29	39	8-9	19(?)	**PT 1 START**
1813	8			41	30	28		40			Pip meets Miss H
c1818?	13				35	33			14-15	25	Mrs Joe attacked
c.1819	14			47	36	34		(46)		26	Pip apprenticed
1820											King George III dies
1823	18	(55)	47-8	51	40	38	40	50	19-20	30	**PT 2 START**
c.1824	19			52	41	39			20-21	31	Mrs Joe dies
1828	23	60	52-3	56	45		45	55	24-5	35	**PT 3 START**
1829	24				c.46				25-6		J&B marry
1830											George IV dies
1837											William IV dies Victoria crowned
1840	36				58				37-38	48	**END (ch.59)**

Place	Significance in the story
Bailey	The Old Bailey. In the 19th century, the Old Bailey was a small court adjacent to Newgate gaol (jail), and named after the street on which it was located. *Real place.*
Barnard's Inn	Where Pip and Herbert lodge when Pip first arrives in London. Originally an Inn of Chancery (a school for law students) by the time in which Great Expectations is set, it had become residential chambers. *Real place.*
Bartholomew Close	Road off Little Britain explored by Pip while waiting for Jaggers. *Real place.*
Battery, the old Battery	A battery is an array of artillery. The 'old battery' would be a disused fort on the north Kent marshes to protect the entrance to the Thames - it has been identified as Cliffe Fort - about 3.3 miles from Cooling. *Real Place*
Billingsgate	London's fish market, seen as Pip and friends row Magwitch down the river in an attempt to escape from England. *Real place*
Blue Boar	A coaching Inn (identified as the Bull Hotel in Rochester) in the nearby town where Pip stays on occasion and catches the London coach.
Botany Bay	Refers to the penal colony in New South Wales, Australia to which convicts (including the fictitious Magwitch) were deported. Though the colony was never actually at the intended Botany Bay, which proved unsuitable, the name stuck. *Real place*
Brentford	Compeyson's House (where Arthur Havisham once stayed) before Compeyson was sent to prison, was in Brentford, now absorbed into West London - about 40 miles from Satis House, but near to Hounslow Heath, where Molly's victim was found. *Real place*
Bridewell	General name given to prisons, after one at St Bride's well in London
Cairo	Egyptian city: site of Clarriker's eastern office where Herbert, and later Pip work. *Real place*
Camberwell Green	Approximate site of Wemmick's wedding to Miss Skiffins Ch. 55. About 1 mile from the 'Castle'. *Real place*
Castle	Wemmick's house in Walworth, (now district of South London) about 2.5 miles from Little Britain (workplace) and Barnard's Inn and Temple (Pip's London dwellings).
Cheapside	Area of London where the Cross Keys is situated. *Real place*
Chelsea Reach	Mentioned by Wemmick to Pip when advising against financial support for Herbert. *Real place*
Chinks Basin	Fictitious location of Old Green Copper Rope-Walk (also fictitious) where Mrs Whimple is Landlady to Mr Barley and Clara, and later Wagwitch (as Mr Campbell).
City	City of London - the old city was entered through gates, of which Newgate, where the prison stood, was one. *Real Place*
Covent Garden	In those days still a fruit and vegetable market. *Real place*
Cross Keys	Coaching inn where Pip joined the coach to Kent, and Estella arrived. It is in Wood Street, Cheapside. It is the place where Dickens arrived in London from Rochester. About 1mile from Barnard's Inn, 1mile from Temple, 11 miles from Richmond, 34 miles by coach from Rochester. *Real place*
Custom House	Used for the collection of duties on the North bank of the Thames and next to London bridge, Pip would pull over here when negotiating the arches of the bridge in his rowing boat became too difficult due to the tide. *Real place.*

Denmark	The country where Hamlet, the play in which Wopsle (as Mr Waldengarver) acted, is set. *Real place.*
Dover	A channel port since Roman times, Dover was the place Pip and Herbert told people his 'uncle' (Magwitch) had gone when he moved to Mrs Whimple. *Real place.*
Epsom	Surrey town famous then as now for horse-racing. Where Magwitch first met Compeyson, at the races. *Real place.*
Erith	A Kentish town on the Southern side of the Thames estuary. While in Lindon, Pip practises his rowing out to Erith - a distance of about 15miles from the Temple stairs on the tidal river. *Real place.*
Essex	County of Essex - the first place Magwitch remembers living. *Real place.*
Essex Street	Street behind Pip's lodgings in Temple where Magwitch is first lodged. *Real place*
Fleet Street	Famous as the home of many printers and publishers (especially of newspapers) in Dickens time, Fleet street would have been a main thoroughfare on Pip's route from his Temple rooms to Little Britain. Pip catches a Hackney cab to the Hummums there. *Real place*
Forge	A blacksmith's workshop, where Joe did his business in Pip's village.
France	Estella stays for several years in France at the same time as Pip is being trained to be a gentleman. *Real place*
Garden Court	Garden Court is Pips Temple address. There is a Garden Court Family Law Chambers just off Essex Street WC2 and Essex St is identified as being just behind Pip's chambers. This is about 0.1 miles from the river, 1mile to Little Britain, 1 mile to Cheapside, 2.5 miles to Walworth, 4 miles to Limehouse (roughly where Magwitch stayed with Mrs Whimple) 5.5 miles to Hammersmith, 10 miles to Richmond. *Real place*
Gerrard Street	Now famous as London's Chinatown, in Dickens' day in was just another largely residential Soho street (Soho hadn't acquired its modern reputation, either). It is where Jaggers apartment is located, convenient for the Old Bailey (and Newgate prison). *Real place.*
Giltspur Street	By Smithfield - Pip parts with Herbert on the corner on way to see Jaggers in Ch. 51, *Real Place.*
Gravesend	Town in North West Kent on the southern bank of the Thames where Pip and friends hole up for the night with Magwitch as they attempt to get him out of England. *Real place*
Greenwich	Wemmick describes the location of Mrs Whimple's house as being 'between Limehouse and Greenwich' in the Pool of London - about 4 miles from Temple and Pip rows out to that point. *Real place.*
Halfway House	A coaching inn/stop on the route from Rochester ('Blue Boar') to the Cross Keys in Cheapside. The Halfway house has been identified as possibly at Welling, in Kent, it is about 20 miles from Rochester and 14 miles from Cheapside. This would make Pip's walk after he stops for breakfast there in Chapter 49 one of twenty miles - something that was not uncommon for Dickens, a great walker, but would still have taken Pip a good six hours. This is consistent, however, with his comment that 'the best light of the day had gone' when he arrived at the town. *Real place (?).*
Hamburg	Major port city in North Germany on the Elba river - one of the destinations for steamers that Pip hoped to get Magwitch onto. *Real place.*

Hammersmith	West London home of Matthew Pocket - about 6 miles from Barnard's Inn, 5.5 miles from Temple, 4.5 miles from Richmond. *Real place.*
Holborn Hill	Mentioned as Wemmick leads Pip from Little Britain to Barnard's Inn. It is now incorporated into the A40 where it crosses Farrington Street. *Real place*
Hounslow Heath	West London heath near where Molly's victim's body was found. *Real place.*
Hulks	Prison ships. A hulk is ship that can float but is not seaworthy - in the case of prison ships, they were usually decommissioned Royal Navy ships. They were particularly used to hold prisoners prior to deportation, such as Magwitch in Great Expectations. There was at least one hulk (HMS Canada) near Chatham on the Medway (next to Rochester) at the time the story is set, but Dickens seems to relocate the hulks in the Thames estuary by the north Kent marshes.
Hummums	A hotel in Covent Garden, the name supposedly deriving from the Arabic 'Hammum' meaning bath, and the hotel offered Turkish bath facilities to travellers. Pip stays there in chapter 45, after being warned not to go home by Wemmick. *Real place.*
Hyde Park	Still wanting to do all he can to make Pip a gentleman, Magwitch advises him to live in the more fashionable Hyde Park area, not the Temple. *Real place.*
Hyde Park Corner	Pip sends 'the Avenger' there from Barnard's Inn - a journey of nearly 2.5miles, to get rid of him for a while (Ch.30). *Real place.*
Kew	Referenced as good neighbourhood for future bride for Alick Pocket to come from (Ch30.) - thus good neighbourhood, between Richmond and Hammersmith. *Real place.*
Limehouse	Wemmick describes the location of Mrs Whimple's house as being 'between Limehouse and Greenwich' - about 4 miles from Temple. *Real place.*
Lime kiln	Landmark for the sluice-house where Orlick lures Pip in Ch.53. A lime kiln is used to heat limestone to produce quicklime - a highly caustic substance. Orlick plans to use the burning kiln to dispose of Pip's body after killing him. Any quarry would have had to have been in the chalk to the west of Pip's village.
Little Britain	London street where Jaggers' office is located, convenient for Old Bailey and Newgate prison. Less than a mile from Barnard's Inn, and maybe a mile and a half from Pip's Temple rooms. About 2 miles from Jaggers' house and 2.5 miles from Wemmick's Walworth home *Real place.*
Liverpool	Wemmick's father worked in warehousing in Liverpool. *Real place*
Lloyds	By the time the novel was set, Lloyds had become the leading global shipping insurer. In Ch. 34, Herbert used to visit the place daily in search of work. *Real place.*
London	England's capital city, where Pip lives after leaving his village and before going overseas. *Real place*
London Bridge	This was the old, medieval London Bridge, which was demolished in 1831. Work on the current London Bridge began in 1825 when Pip was about 20, about two years after arriving in London. At some states of the tide Pip could not negotiate the eddying water under the arches and had to come ashore. (Ch. 47) *Real place at the time of writing*

Marseilles	Mediterranean port city in southern France where Herbert is away on business when Magwitch comes to find Pip at his Temple address (Ch.39) *Real place*
Mill Pond Bank	Fictitious location of the (fictitious) Old Green Copper Rope Walk where Magwitch stayed prior to the attempt to leave England.
Newgate	London's main gaol (jail), and by the time Pip is there, the place of execution (by hanging). Although there had been a prison there since the twelfth century, the building Dickens knew dated from 1872. Situated on the corner of Newgate Street and Old Bailey, it was closed in 1902 and demolished two years later. It was only a five minute walk from Jaggers' office, and Wemmick takes Pip there on a visit. *Real place.*
New South Wales	Now an Australian state, then it was the name given by Captain Cook to a British colony in South East Australia in which Botany Bay is located. Jaggers is careful to 'not know' that Magwitch is back in England by repeatedly referring to him as being in New South Wales. *Real place.*
Old Green Copper Rope Walk	Fictitious address for Mrs Whimple and guests.
Portsmouth	Hampshire port city where Magwitch landed on return to England as Provis. *Real place*
Richmond	Surrey town (now incorporated into greater London) where Estella lived in Mrs Brandley's house: about 10 miles from Temple, 4.5 miles from Hammersmith and 11.5 miles from the Cross Keys (Cheapside) *Real place.*
Rotterdam	Major port city in South Holland - one of the destinations for steamers that Pip hoped to get Magwitch onto. *Real place.*
Satis House	The fictional home of Miss Havisham, Satis means 'enough' as in 'satisfied' (had enough). Although the town where Satis House is situated is not named, it is based on Rochester in Kent. Pip's village is believed to be based on Cooling, which is about 6.5 miles away. (The forge is given as 4 miles from Pumblechook's shop – Ch. 8)
Shropshire	Pip, in Ch. 42 compares Kent to Bentley Drummle's Shropshire, although in Ch.25 he is stated to come from Somersetshire. It is not clear if this is a mistake. *Real place.*
Smithfield	Dickens is referring to Smithfield market, London's ancient meat market: " all asmear with filth and fat and blood and foam". Pip goes there when exploring while awaiting his first appointment with Jaggers, a five minute walk from Little Britain. *Real place.*
Somersetshire	Pip, in Ch. 42 compares Kent to Bentley Drummle's Shropshire, although in Ch.25 he is stated to come from Somersetshire. It is not clear if this is a mistake. *Real place.*
St Pauls	St Pauls cathedral overlooks Little Britain and is seen by Pip as he explores while waiting for Jaggers. (Ch.20) *Real place*
Temple	Pip and Herbert move to Garden Court in the Temple area of London in the time that elapses between chapters 38 and 39. This is quite close to the Temple stairs down to the river, where the Wellington is now moored, and from where Pip sometimes set off on his rowing trips. *Real place*
The Pool	The Poole of London is the name given to the stretch of river between London Bridge and Limehouse. The Limehouse end is the area in which Mrs. Whimple's house is, near the river. *Real place*
The Ship	Inn on the river where Pip, Herbert, Magwitch and Startop spend the night as they attempt to get Magwitch out of England. There is a pub

	called *The Ship and Lobster* on the river bank at Gravesend which might be the inspiration. Gravesend is about 14 miles downriver from Limehouse, where Magwitch was staying.
Three Jolly Bargemen	Pip's village is normally identified as being based on Cooling, 6.5 miles north of Rochester. This would suggest that the Three Jolly Bargemen might be based on The Horseshoe and Castle, Cooling, which has been there since at least 1835, although the original wooden clapboard building (which Dickens would have known) burned down in about 1915 and was rebuilt in brick. The Three Jolly Bargemen is Joe's local, where (amongst other events) he meets the man who slips Pip £2 from Magwitch, where Joe was when Mrs Joe was attacked and where Jaggers finds Joe and Pip.
Traitor's Gate	The river gate of the tower of London, passed on the flight down the Thames with Magwitch. *Real place*
Walworth	A southern suburb of London (South of the Thames) where Wemmick lives with his Aged Parent in his wooden 'Castle'. The Old Kent Road (now the A2) runs through Walworth, and might incidentally have been the route Pip travelled to Rochester. 'Walworth' also represents the more playful side of Wemmick's nature which he does not allow to surface when in Jagger's office. *Real place.*
Westminster Abbey	Pip and Herbert go to church at Westminster Abbey in Ch.22 - Pip's only recorded act of church-going as an adult. About 2.5 miles from Barnard's Inn. *Real place.*
Whitefriars	Pip approaches the Temple by the Whitefriars gate in after walking dejectedly back from Satis House (30 miles - a 10 hour walk!) chapter 44 *Real place*
White Tower	The old keep of the tower of London, passed on the flight down the Thames with Magwitch. *Real place*
Woolsack	The woolsack is the seat, in the House of Lords, of the Lord Chancellor, the senior law officer - so when Pip observes in Ch. 23 that Mr Pocket in his youth had "not quite decided whether to mount to the Woolsack, or to roof himself in with a mitre" he is suggesting that Mr. Pocket had expected to rise easily to the top of either the law or the church (bishop's mitre).

Content quiz– how well do you know the story in Part 1? Try this **multiple choice** test:

Question:	A	B	C	Answer:
Sample: Pip got his name because…	…he couldn't say 'Philip Pirrip'.	…Miss Havisham gave him the name.	… His secret benefactor insisted he keep it.	A
1] Pip's family are…	…all dead.	…his sister and her husband, Mr & Mrs Joe Gargery.	…well known in the area as they work in the churchyard.	
2] The man in the cemetery…	…wanted to eat Pip.	…wanted food and a file.	… to escape by taking Pip hostage.	
3] Mrs Joe Gargery…	… regularly beat both Pip and Joe.	… had flaxen curls.	… was almost 20 years older than Pip.	
4] Tickler was…	… a game the family loved playing.	… a wax-tipped cane.	… a family friend.	
5] On Christmas morning…	… Pip realised he hadn't slept at all.	… Pip got up early, hoping for presents.	… Pip imagined the floorboards shouting, 'Stop thief!	
6] On the way to keep his promise, Pip…	…imagined the cows shouting, 'Stop thief!	… was attacked by a different convict.	… lost his way slightly, going too far right.	
7] At the Christmas meal, Pip was …	…laughing about Wopsle's big nose.	… terrified his theft would be discovered.	… handcuffed as he tried to run away.	
8] The soldiers needed Joe to…	… fix the lock on their handcuffs.	… light a warm fire for them - it was freezing.	… help them search for the convicts.	
9] The convict does a very kind thing for Pip…	… when he says he believes Pip didn't tell on him.	… by claiming to have stolen a Pork pie and brandy.	… by fighting the man who wanted to eat his liver.	
10] Pip continued to feel bad about stealing the food…	…because he had fat cheeks, but they were hungry now.	…only because everyone was talking about it.	… because he felt Joe would never trust him again if he knew.	
11] When Pip discovers Joe can't read, he also…	…discovers why Joe never challenges his wife.	… how he used to work for Miss Havisham instead of going to school.	…hears she's going to work for the government.	
12] When Pip goes to 'play' at Miss Havisham's, he notices at once…	… that all the clocks have stopped.	…that the house is called 'Satis', which is Latin for 'enough'	…that Estella, though his own age, is very scornful of him and calls him 'boy'.	
13] Pip tells Miss Havisham in her ear that…	… his sister will beat him if she doesn't invite him back in the future.	… that Estella is proud, pretty and insulting.	…he wants to go home, but wouldn't mind seeing Estella again.	

14] A stranger, in the *Three Jolly Bargemen*, gave Pip…	… rum and water stirred with a file.	…a shilling wrapped in two one pound notes.	…news of Magwitch.	
15] Pip first met Jaggers at Miss Havisham's …	…on her birthday when all the Pockets were visiting.	…on his first visit to her when Estella took him upstairs.	…on the day he became apprenticed to Joe.	
16] Pip first met Matthew Pocket…	…in London.	…Miss Havisham's room playing with Estella.	…when he challenged him to a boxing match at Satis House.	
17] Pip's indentures of apprenticeship to Joe were paid for by…	…Miss Havisham.	…Mr Jaggers.	…Magwitch.	
18] "It is a most miserable thing…	"… to love a beautiful woman."	"… to work at a forge."	"…to feel ashamed of home."	
19] When Orlick said, You'd be everybody's master, if you durst," he was talking about…	… Pip, who wanted a half-holiday to visit Miss Havisham.	… Joe, who knocked him down into the coal-dust.	… that "foul shrew," he called "mother Gargery".	
20] On the day Pip visited Miss Havisham, he discovered…	… that his convict had escaped again.	… that Estella was being educated abroad.	… that his sister had been killed by an intruder.	
21] Pip's sister had been attacked with…	… Magwitch's filed off leg-iron.	…Orlick's hammer.	…Joe's file.	
22] Pip says to himself, "Pip, what a fool you are," because…	… he let Orlick walk home with him and Biddy though she didn't like him.	…he suspected that Orlick had killed his sister.	… he knew that Estella would make him unhappy, yet he still pined for her.	
23] In the fourth year of his apprenticeship, Pip met Jaggers again when…	…he visited Miss Havisham.	… he asked for Joe at the *Three Jolly Bargemen*.	… he knocked on the kitchen door one night.	
24] When Pip thought about having a fortune, he began to wonder…	…whether "Miss Havisham intended me for Estella".	…whether he should bestow, "a dinner of roast beef and plum pudding" on everyone in the church.	…whether he should buy Joe a new house.	
25] After his rise to fortune, Pip was called "my dear young Friend" by…	…Joe.	…Orlick	…Pumblechook.	

Content quiz– how well do you know the story in Part 2?

Name the person:

Sample: Who kept interrupting a meal to shake hands with Pip, having tormented him as a boy, but now claiming to be "the humble instrument" of Pip's good fortune?   **Pumblechook**

1] Who "had the same air of knowing something to everybody else's disadvantage, as his master had."?

2] Who was "the pale young gentleman"?

3] Who is Pip's guardian?

4] Who is Handel?

5] Who received a letter "...when she was dressing for her marriage"?

6] Who is "...in a counting-house and looking about me"?

7] Who "was a gentleman with a rather perplexed expression on his face..."?

8] Who is "...an old looking young man of a heavy order of architecture..."?

9] Who refers to herself as "... grandpapa's granddaughter"?

10] Whose mouth is described as "a slit" that food is "posted" into?

11] Who says, "I am...my own Jack of all Trades."?

12] Who is known as "the Aged"?

13] Whom did Jaggers call "the spider"?

14] Who has the "delicate face"?

15] Whose face looked "...all disturbed by fiery air"?

16] His Hamlet had the audience –Pip included- laughing; he stayed with Pip till 2am after an invitation to supper – what is his real name?

17] Who wore green gloves all evening on a visit to Walworth?

18] Who says "It's death to come back..."?

19] Who sets out to, "deceive and entrap." Bentley Drummle?

20] Who does Pip guiltily feel he has "deserted"?

Content quiz– how well do you know the story in Part 3?

Complete the quote:

1] "Take nothing on its …..; take everything on …"

2] "I've been locked up, as much as…"

3] "Surely I had seen exactly such … and such …., on a memorable occasion very lately!"

4] "…until I saw you in a looking-glass that showed me what …, I did not know what I had done."

5] "…she is a lady and very …. And I…..her!"

Answers:

Part 1

1 B	**2** B	**3** A	**4** B	**5** C	**6** C	**7** B	**8** A
9 B	**10** C	**11** A	**12** C	**13** B	**14** B	**15** A	**16** C
17 A	**18** C	**19** C	**20** B	**21** A	**22** C	**23** B	**24** A
25 C							

Part 2

1 Wemmick	**2** Herbert Pocket	**3** Jaggers	**4** Pip	**5** Miss Havisham
6 Herbert Pocket	**7** Matthew Pocket	**8** Bentley Drummle	**9** Mrs Belinda Pocket	**10** John Wemmick
11 Wemmick	**12** Wemmick's father	**13** Bentley Drummle	**14** Startop	**15** Molly, Jaggers' housekeeper
16 Mr Wopsle	**17** Miss Skiffins	**18** Magwitch/ Provis	**19** Estella	**20** Joe

Part 3

1] looks; evidence   2] a silver tea-kettle   3] eyes, hands

4] I once felt myself   5] beautiful; love

70

Assessment Objectives & Exam questions:

Several exam boards offer *Great Expectations* as a text for their literature exam: AQA, OCR & Edexel.

All the exam boards have the same **Assessment Objectives** [AOs], 1-4:

AO1 Read, understand and respond to texts. Students should be able to: • maintain a critical style and develop an informed personal response • use textual references, including quotations, to support and illustrate interpretations.

AO2 Analyse the language, form and structure used by a writer to create meanings and effects, using relevant subject terminology where appropriate.

AO3 Show understanding of the relationships between texts and the contexts in which they were written.

AO4 Use a range of vocabulary and sentence structures for clarity, purpose and effect, with accurate spelling and punctuation.

What this means:

AO1 – **Know the whole story**, so that you can mention other relevant events or characters. This is **reference**.

   - All the exam boards offer an extract: use relevant **quotes** from there and learn a few key quotes [just phrases] that could be relevant to several questions – character descriptions are particularly adaptable.

   - Link what you write to the task set and keep showing how Dickens is achieving a purpose. This is what is meant by **'maintaining a critical style'**. Don't just re-tell the story!

AO2 - **language**: Discuss **imagery, language** that creates a **mood or** highlights an **attitude** in a character. Mention other **possible interpretations** of the language. Are there a series of **verbs** denoting action, for example, or lots of **adjectives** that emphasise the same thing? When you write about what effect Dickens achieves by using them, you'll be writing about language.

   - **form**: *Great Expectations* is a **novel** first written in **serial** form. When you write about the use of **dialogue** in a passage, or detailed **descriptions** being used to slow the pace of a passage, you're writing about form. Are **opposites** being focused on, or does the way the extract is written **contrast** in style with other chapters, for example if characters speak simply, whereas in other chapters they are more verbose [wordy]?

   - **structure**:   When you say **what came before** your extract or chapter and **what it is preparing the reader for**, you're writing about structure. What effect does Dickens achieve by revealing information in the order he chooses, e.g. building suspense, **foreshadowing** etc. What has **changed** from the start of the extract/chapter to the end, how has the story or character been developed?

AO3 – Context is the **background information** that helps the reader **orientate** the story. When you mention things that affect Dickens' work and the reader's response to it, you are writing about context. Only mention contextual information where it is relevant to the task/extract: <u>do not tag it on as a paragraph of facts</u>, only weave it in to explain attitudes or expectations.

If relevant, refer to:

Dicken's own life e.g. his changed financial & social situation, that he'd spent part of his youth in Kent, so knew the marshes well,

the **historical** setting, i.e. Victorian era, and **location** i.e. Kent & London, suggesting how this might influence the story,

social and **cultural** contexts e.g., attitudes in society, for example the way criminals were shipped off to Australia with no hope of returning to Britain, or that women like Estella were expected to make financially advantageous marriages; expectations of different cultural groups, like the fact that the classes were supposed to keep to their own place and dress differently

the **literary** context of the text, for example, literary movements or genres: in the nineteenth century novel the lives of ordinary people are also of interest to readers,

the way in which **texts are received and engaged with** by different audiences, at different times, for example, how a text may be **read differently** in the twenty-first century from when it was written – today the upbringing Miss Havisham submitted Estella to would be illegal in Britain rather than 'romantic'; Pip's change of fortune would not be quite so unusual etc.

AO4 – Accuracy and **style:** this is something to work on well before the exam!

NB *There are often no specific marks for AO4 in this task, but it does affect the level at which the other AOs are judged, so don't neglect it!*

Some tips for improving are:

- **Spell** names **correctly** – learn them, using memory aids if necessary. Also learn the spelling of key terms you will be likely to use, for example 'characterisation'. Breaking words up into their root word, prefix and suffix often helps, as does finding words within words or creating mnemonics.

- **Plan work**! Cluster together ideas that focus on the same thing and order your clusters. Check that what you plan to say does address the question and that you're including some possible interpretations or issues open to debate if you want top marks.

- **Opening** with a **short paragraph** which gives **the 'short answer' to the question** – what you'd say if the question was only worth 2-4 marks – is a good way of stating your overarching point, the one you plan to explain and prove. Another effective opening is **placing the extract in its structural context** – say what has just happened in the relevant story thread before this and what the writer is preparing the reader for here.

- **Quote** from the text at least a few times to give **evidence** of what you claim. You can also **refer** to events, putting them in your own words. <u>Do not make up quotes</u> – the examiners know the texts! It is easier to remember some key phrases and words, rather than long quotes. **Embed** [insert] these quoted words and phrases in your sentences, making sure you use **quotation marks** so that they can be awarded marks for being quoted on purpose.

- **Linking** the **'steps' of your argument** to each other by using connectives ['However'] or discourse markers ['Next'] gives your work clarity. It is also vital to link what you write **to the task**, so that it is obvious that what you say actually does engage with the task set.

Wording of questions:

Each exam board [aka awarding body] has its own style, but all provide an extract. If you are unsure whose exam you are doing, ask your teacher. Each board provides an example of how the question will be formulated. There are **examples on the specimen material** supplied by each board to your teacher, which for copyright reasons we can't quote. However, here is the **type of question** they will ask, this is more or less how they will formulate or word the task:

Read/ Explore/ Use the following **extract** from Chapter .... of *Great Expectations* and **then answer the question that follows**. In this extract, ...[*here they briefly summarise that the extract is about*]

The extract that follows is about 15 to 30 lines long.

Starting with this extract, **write about how Dickens presents ideas about …** in *Great Expectations*. Write about: • what … says about … in **this extract** • how Dickens presents ideas about … **in the novel as a whole**. [… marks – usually 30; 40; or 20 + 20]

The 'trick' is to do your close reading and quoting mainly from the extract - which you have in front of you- linking what you find to the rest of the novel by referring from memory to key characters, moments or examples as you develop your point. However, you may be asked to answer is two stages for 20 + 20 marks. In that case, focus on each stage separately.

Here are examples of other formulations:

• **Explore how Dickens presents ideas about** … through the presentation of …, in **this extract and elsewhere in the novel**. [… marks] In this extract, ...[*here they briefly summarise that the extract is about*]

NB *This exam board is the only one to offer an option that follows a separate form: it has one question that asks you to consider the whole novel, but focus on 2 episodes or 'moments' in the novel. No extract is given. This is an optional question, so you do **either** A **or** B*

• **Use this extract** to answer Question …. *Great Expectations*: Charles Dickens. In Chapter …..[*here they briefly summarise that the extract is about*] The extract follows…

Question …. – *Great Expectations* (a) Explore **how Dickens presents …'s thoughts and feelings about** … in this extract. **Give examples from the extract to support your ideas.**   (20 marks)

(b) In this extract, …'s … is shown. Explain … **elsewhere in the novel.** In your answer you must consider: • how… • the effect on … (20 marks) (Total for Question …. = 40 marks)

To summarise:

All the exam boards have a question that follows this format in more or less the same way:

1] an extract is given, with a brief description of what it is about.

2] a question is set about a theme or character in the novel

3] you have to use the extract to write about the theme using quotes from the extract – 'close reading', then you need to relate what you glean from the extract to the text as a whole – *how does Dickens develop these ideas in the rest of the novel?*

4] there are two main types of extract question:

 'How Dickens presents ideas about'… - these are **thematic** questions, about themes.

'How Dickens presents ……'s thoughts and feelings about…' the development of …'s character in the rest of the novel – these are **character** questions.

The next step is to practise some questions, so find a quiet place to work, get pen, paper and some sort of timing device so that you can begin to answer within the time limits set by your particular exam board.

Answering an exam question:

1] Planning:

You won't cover all the AOs by accident, so make sure you have something to say about each of them from the planning stage.

Use a highlighter to pick out your quotes and annotate the points you'll make on the extract – you are allowed to write on your question paper.

As you annotate, think of relevant links to the rest of the novel and jot them down too.

This might be a good 'plan' format to have in your head (but use what works for you!):

AO – ask what is relevant to…	Extract	Rest of the novel

1 Themes & characters
   Your opinion - justified
   Other interpretations		

2 Language
   Structure
   Form		

3 Victorian era,
   Dickens,
   Difference in attitude of
readers then and now…		

4 Check spelling, especially of character names; use correct terms; use PEEL or similar in paragraphs with a clear topic sentence, quoted evidence or references, explanations that explore, expand and analyse as well as evaluate and link tour points to the task and the paragraph to the next step in your answer with connectives.

Let's try planning

Explore how Dickens presents ideas about social class in this extract and elsewhere in *Great Expectations.*

In this extract from the end of chapter 27, Joe has come to visit Pip in London and the visit has not gone well. Joe is saying goodbye to Pip. As a start, think about:

• what Joe says about social class in this extract

• how Dickens presents ideas about social class in the novel as a whole.

"Pip, dear old chap, life is made of ever so many partings welded together, as I may say, and one man's a blacksmith, and one's a whitesmith, and one's a goldsmith, and one's a coppersmith. Diwisions among such must come, and must be met as they come. If there's been any fault at all to-day, it's mine. You and me is not two figures to be together in London; nor yet anywheres else but what is private, and beknown, and understood among friends. It ain't that I am proud, but that I want to be right, as you shall never see me no more in these clothes. I'm wrong in these clothes. I'm wrong out of the forge, the kitchen, or off th' meshes. You won't find half so much fault in me if you think of me in my forge dress, with my hammer in my hand, or even my pipe. You won't find half so much fault in me if, supposing as you should ever wish to see me, you come and put your head in at the forge window and see Joe the blacksmith, there, at the old anvil, in the old burnt apron, sticking to the old work. I'm awful dull, but I hope I've beat out something nigh the rights of this at last. And so GOD bless you, dear old Pip, old chap, GOD bless you!"

I had not been mistaken in my fancy that there was a simple dignity in him. The fashion of his dress could no more come in its way when he spoke these words, than it could come in its way in Heaven. He touched me gently on the forehead, and went out.

AO – ask what is relevant to…	Extract	Rest of the novel
1 Themes & characters Your opinion - justified Other interpretations		
2 Language Structure Form		
3 Victorian era, Dickens,		

Difference in attitude of readers then and now…		

4 Check spelling, especially of character names; use correct terms; use PEEL or similar in paragraphs with a clear topic sentence, quoted evidence or references, explanations that explore, expand and analyse as well as evaluate and link tour points to the task and the paragraph to the next step in your answer with connectives.

Let's check planning:

Explore how Dickens presents ideas about social class in this extract and elsewhere in *Great Expectations*.

In this extract from the end of chapter 27, Joe has come to visit Pip in London and the visit has not gone well. Joe is saying goodbye to Pip. As a start, think about:

• what Joe says about social class in this extract

• how Dickens presents ideas about social class in the novel as a whole.

metaphorical language reflects Joe's trade

"Pip, dear old chap, life is made of ever so many partings welded together, as I may say, and one man's a blacksmith, and one's a whitesmith, and one's a goldsmith, and one's a coppersmith. Diwisions among such must come, and must be met as they come. If there's been any fault at all to-day, it's mine. You and me is not two figures to be together in London; nor yet anywheres else but what is private, and beknown, and understood among friends. It ain't that I am proud, but that I want to be right, as you shall never see me no more in these clothes. I'm wrong in these clothes. I'm wrong out of the forge, the kitchen, or off th' meshes. You won't find half so much fault in me if you think of me in my forge dress, with my hammer in my hand, or even my pipe. You won't find half so much fault in me if, supposing as you should ever wish to see me, you come and put your head in at the forge window and see Joe the blacksmith there, at the old anvil, in the old burnt apron, to the old work. I'm awful dull, but I hope I've beat out something nigh the rights of this at last. And so GOD bless you, dear old Pip, old chap, GOD bless you!"

I had not been mistaken in my fancy that there was a simple dignity in him. The fashion of his dress could no more come in its way when he spoke these words, than it could come in its way in Heaven. He touched me gently on the forehead, and went out.

Joe's conservative views, reflect early Victorian beliefs about social position.

Type of work suggests social class- physical rather

Metaphor reflects Joe's trade.

Repetition of 'old' to denote fondness & familiarity.

Pip's reference to his own snobbery.

AO – ask what is relevant to...	Extract	Rest of the novel
1 Themes & characters Your opinion - justified Other interpretations	- Joe's wisdom about social class and his place in it: 'I'm wrong...' - relationship between Joe and Pip and how Joe is shown to care for Pip	How attitudes towards social class are shown in a different part of the novel e.g. Bentley Drummle's snide remarks about seeing 'smithies' on his ride in the countryside.
2 Language Structure Form	- Use of tools and clothing as metaphors for social position; - word 'old' to suggest both fondness and the status quo – Joe's ideas are the conservative Victorian ones. - Presentation of Joe's character in this extract, in particular as used to highlight Pip's snobbery and pretension - Joe's language, such as how the fluency of speech contrasts with the dialect words and phrasing – 'off th'meshes'- and highlights his inherent wisdom.	- Compare Pip's attitudes at this point in the novel to a later point when his character has learned wisdom e.g. when he meets Magwitch - Compare Pip's treatment of Joe to Estella's scorn of the young Pip and how differently they re-act: Joe is content to be who he is. - Compare Pip's treatment of Joe to Matthew's kindness in teaching him manners without being judgemental.
3 Victorian era, Dickens, Difference in attitude of readers then and now...	- Many Victorians believed God had ordained [intended] your place in society, so it was disobedient to aim higher. - Joe's feelings about the lack of fluidity of social class e.g 'sticking to the old work' - social class was related to work: a gentleman shouldn't work - Joe's acknowledgement of Pip's judgement and how it is formed by his attempt to behave and dress 'out of his class'	Dickens explores – and had experience of – how money esp. debt, makes a difference to social status. Matthew is a gentleman, but poverty makes him have to work, whereas Bentley has the money to lead a gentleman's life, has the position, but not the manners- Orlick could be seen as his low-status counterpart.
4 Check spelling, especially of character names; use correct terms; use PEEL or similar in paragraphs with a clear topic sentence, quoted evidence or references, explanations that explore, expand and analyse as well as evaluate and link tour points to the task and the paragraph to the next step in your answer with connectives.		

You won't have time in an exam to write all this down, but by doing so when you practise, you develop the right habits of thinking. Even annotating the text is less detailed, just write a key word to remind you of your thoughts. So your plan may, in reality, look more like this:

AO 1 - gulf betw'n classes - J: 'wrong' out've wrk clothes

2 - lang. - wrk - status; frm - J's farewell speech [most he's said]

3 - Vic atts chng - s. stus god-ordained; evn gentlemen [Matt. P] wk fr liv'n; D's own life

2] Structuring your answer:

There are three components to your essay -

a] the short answer – this provides the over-arching point you 'prove' in the essay

b] something to cover each AO

c] your own thoughts, opinions and possible interpretations, either in conclusion or woven in

Let's try structuring an essay:

a] Here are 3 possible openings – choose the one you like the most and develop it or write your own:

This extract explores the concept of what a gentleman really is: Joe, with the lower social status, is more of a gentleman in his behaviour than Pip...

OR

Because of his father's recurring debt and then his own raised status as a famous writer, Dickens understood what it was like to change social class at a time when the prevailing thought was that God had decided what class you should be and you ought to stay there.

OR

In this extract Pip shows how his new status has turned him into a snob and the Pip who narrates the events in the extract now feels very ashamed of his behaviour.

b] Covering the AOs:

AO1 - **AO3** : see table above and add your own ideas. Don't write about the AOs separately, because some things, like 'I'm wrong in these clothes' cover several AOs – explore them all as you analyse and evaluate the effectiveness of the quote.

To cover **AO4**, check your work for accurate spelling, clear paragraphing, connectives that make your line of argument clear and embedded quotes.

Here are 3 possible endings – choose the one you like the most and put it in your own words:

3] *I think that Dickens is making Pip's behaviour echo Estella's – her snobbery made Pip ashamed of himself, his rough hands and the way he called the 'knaves' 'Jacks'; in contrast, Joe does not feel ashamed of himself, he just sadly realises that away from the common ground of the forge, he and Pip are now divided by their social status.*

OR

This meeting foreshadows Pip's meeting with Magwitch and I think because of learning his lesson with Joe, Pip is more understanding than he would have been when Magwitch reveals who he is.

OR

Perhaps what makes Pip so annoyed with Joe is that his visit is like a mirror through which Pip sees himself as he must have looked to Matthew when he first arrived in London. Joe reminds him that he is not a true gentleman, merely an overdressed 'common labouring-boy'.

Now write your essay. Set the time limit your exam board suggests.

Here is an essay written in the time limit of 45minutes, without a text. Read it and decide how successfully you think it has answered the question. What has been done well, what could be improved? Annotate the AOs you spot and comment on features.

Here is an essay written in the time limit of 45minutes, without a text. Read it and decide how successfully you think it has answered the question. What has been done well, what could be improved?

Dickens uses Joe's visit to show what a snob Pip has become, as well as to link the past- Estella's snobbery towards him – with the future: his acceptance of Magwitch as his benefactor is made possible by what he learns this encounter with Joe.

Just as Pip had to get new clothes for his move to London, Joe has been dressed up – presumably also by Trabb- with ridiculously high points to his collar, for his visit. The obviously uncomfortable new clothes – and his constantly falling hat- become a focus for Pip's resentment of his former companion and a symbol of Joe's efforts to make himself worthy of Pip's new social status. So when Joe say: "I'm wrong in these clothes", he is actually talking about being wrong in London, in Pip's new life and in trying to socialise with a gentleman. Their true friendship, he realises, can only be restored in the forge, where he is "Joe the blacksmith" in the "old burnt apron" at the "old anvil".

The repetition of the word "old" serves two functions. Firstly, it suggests a fondness for the familiar things – likewise evidenced by Dickens's use of metaphors that reflect Joe's trade: partings 'welded', thoughts 'beat out'. But it also emphasises Joe's conservatism- he sticks to the "old" ways. Many Victorians believed that your social status was God ordained and to wish for more was inviting trouble – Biddy and Joe represent this way of thinking. They believe contentment is found by accepting your lot.

However, the Victorian era was also a time of "self-help", when workers were encouraged to learn to read and write to better themselves; Dickens is ambiguous about this: both Pip and Joe learn to read and write, thanks in large part to Biddy.

In addition, Dicken himself had experience of moving from one social status to another- downwardly mobile when his father's debt caused him to have to leave school and work in a blacking factory and upwardly mobile through his own successful career.

Though Dicken's message on social status may be debatable – Joe's story after all has a happier ending than Pip's – it is clear that Magwitch, who has sponsored Pip's rise in status, is able to benefit from the insight Pip has gained through this meeting with Joe.

The forge, the kitchen, the "meshes", "with my hammer in my hand" is where he can be "Joe the blacksmith", in that private world of the two companions that have faced the "tickler". "You and me is not two figures to be together in London", Joe admits, but only because of Pip's own snobbery. Matthew finds no fault with Joe; Pip was once like Joe. So perhaps it is social pretension that Dickens exposes so harshly here. Pretending makes Pip hyper-sensitive to the social inequality represented by Joe.

In this extract, Dickens has given Joe a long, eloquent speech, which contracts with the colloquial language he uses and with the character Pip's silence. Pip the narrator, looking back, comments on Joe's dignity. I think Dickens wants us to recognise in Joe's wisdom that he is the truer "gentleman".

Another contrast is between Pip's boyhood reaction to Estella's scorn – he felt deeply ashamed of his social class and therefore uncomfortable at the forge – and Joe's reaction to Pip's scorn. Joe decides to return to where he belongs, ever a friend, never an intruder. When Pip loses his social status as a result of losing his fortune, Joe is there to look after him, to serve. But as Pip recovers, he steps back, content to let Pip find his way in the world.

Maybe what Dickens is showing readers is that social class is shallow: true "class" comes from within. After all, Bentley Drummle and Orlick are two of a kind...

Try again: Here is another essay written under the same conditions. How does it compare? Take what you like best from these two and use it in your own practice.

By presenting Joe Gargery as a sympathetic character, Dickens questions the established Victorian notions of wealth and class, and what effects they have on being a gentleman.

Joe Gargery is very much working class and his language is very much tied in with his trade. Metaphors such as 'life is made of ever so many partings welded together' – along with his colloquial speech - show that he has little education outside the confines of his job. However he still shows a deep thoughtfulness and compassion ('God bless you old Pip') that is a far cry from the ignorant and bawdy lower class stereotype that pervaded the upper class Victorian imagination.

Even though he acknowledges his own low birth – ' I'm wrong in these clothes'- he is better mannered and kinder than the wealthier 'gentleman', Pip; an inversion of the stereotypes which to modern audiences almost seems stereotypical in itself (i.e. the idea that rich people are snobbish), but at the time (to Dickens's first readers) would have been far more shocking.

Therefore, the contrast between Joe and Pip, and in particular the presentation of Joe as caring and thoughtful, constitutes one way in which Dickens presents ideas about class in Great Expectations.

However, though Joe in some ways defies class stereotypes, the way Dickens has tied his language with his job also seems to imply that his class is who he is and is thus unavoidable; which ties in to the Victorian belief that classes were ordained by God and should not be defied. Biddy seems to imply this when she responds so coolly to Pip's request that she help Joe to improve his language skills so that he can try to 'raise him up' when he has come into his fortune.

Perhaps the story of Pip's inability to fit in with high society is intended as a moral tale about the dangers of social ambition... although since Dickens himself had risen considerably in wealth since his birth, this seems unlikely.

Regardless, Joe's constant references to smithing: 'one man's blacksmith', 'my hammer in my hand' and 'I'm wrong out of my forge' make him sound almost caricaturish in his inability to talk of anything other than his job. In this way Dickens seems to present the view that wealth and class determine personality and are inherent to members of those classes. Apart from Biddy, the characters of Pip's youth all seem to be verbose, as Joe is here, obscuring the message by their words rather than speaking plainly.

Elsewhere in the novel though, Dickens seems to imply that the lack of social mobility and Pip's struggle to fit in are perpetuated by the Victorian belief in class boundaries. As the narrator, Pip also serves as the protagonist and the reader supports him in his plight. Therefore, the snobbery and scorn Pip gets for his low birth – from characters like Drummle – doesn't seem righteous or divinely ordained: it seems unfair. Dickens presents the lack of social mobility as unfair, but also notes how self-perpetuating it is; hence Pip's snobbery towards Joe Gargery in the extract.

In conclusion, Dickens presents views about social class by playing with and subverting stereotypes and expectations to challenge the cultural norms of Victorian Britain.

Now think about how you could improve this answer. Ask your teacher for a copy of your exam board's generic mark-scheme, or look on line for one they make available [under literature, the 19th century novel]- it always helps to know what your specific board wants, but they are more or less the same, focusing on the AOs. Weaker answers throw out bits of information, stronger ones build a cohesive [fitted together/ organised] argument and the best have an element of debate, possible interpretations and some evaluation of the effect on the reader or the writer's purpose as well.

In this extract Dickens writes very well to draw the reader in. Firstly there are lists: blacksmith, whitesmith, goldsmith and coppersmiths- all these words sound like the beat of a hammer. Joe is a blacksmith. Another list is 'my hammer, my hand, my pipe, and lastly old anvil, old apron and 'old work'. This lists is to make it true when Joe quotes: 'I'm awful dull but I hope I beat out something.'

Joe believes in God and says god bless you twice. This is repetition, to be like goodbye e.g. god-by-you. More Victorians did believe in God so Joe says God bless. He is leaving because Pip is a gentleman now and Joe has to go back to the forge and all his old stuff but Pips is new because Jaggers gave him money to buy new clothes. I think this is a good description of Joe who is still poor and Pip who is rich 'not two figures to be in London' and because the hammer sounds are clever.

Although there are some good ideas about Dickens's purpose in using lists and repetition here which might be insightful in a stronger candidate, a generous examiner could award no more than a mid-level 2 for this answer.

There is no sense that the question is being answered at all. There is 'some awareness' of some elements in the extract, but not how they show how Dickens presents ideas about social class.

Nor does the candidate engage with Joe's views on the matter social class. AO1 is not met as the rest of the novel is not discussed and while the language element of AO2 is touched on, it is not linked to the task. The contextual information –AO3- is irrelevant.

Sadly, similar candidates often leave the exams feeling they have done well because they have - in their own minds- written about all the AOs. This is why a good way to start your essay answer is with the short answer. Then you have engaged with the actual task. From there it is easier to make your next steps actually 'proving' that answer by quoting from the text. Write about each quote in more detail, explaining its relevance [NB **not explaining the quote, but why it is evidence**!] and referring to other places in the novel where the same – or the opposite – is true. Then link the point you've made to the next point with a connective, or say how it answers the question.

The bottom line is:

Begin correctly and the next steps fall more naturally into place.

> Open with 'the short answer'
>
> Prove it using PEEL/ PEAL while covering AO1, AO2 & AO3
>
> End with a brief, final opinion.

Good luck and I 'OPE you do very well in the exams!

[1] Kent is never specifically named as the county of *Pip*'s village or the nearby town, but the town is clearly based on Rochester in north Kent, a place very familiar to Dickens and the village is generally identified as being largely based on the nearby village of Cooling.

[2] The passage of time is difficult to track. Dickens notes say that *Pip* is about seven at the start of the story, and a year passes between chapters six and seven. Another year, or thereabouts, is mentioned as passing in chapter twelve - but he is old enough to be apprenticed at the end of chapter twelve, and this was normally at age fourteen - indeed we are told in chapter 18 that he was released from his indentures in the fourth year of his apprenticeship - and he seems to be about eighteen when he goes up to London. Maybe chapter twelve actually spans six years, but this is not clear.

[3] The time is identified as half past two - two hours would take the time to 4.30, and sunset is at about 4.00pm - the clocks must have been an hour different to our current regime, with sunset at 5.00pm, which would have made first light, when *Pip* went out to the convict, close to 9.00am

[4] Education wasn't compulsory in England until 1880 - then for 5-10 year olds.

[5] According to Dickens' notes, in part three of the book *Miss Havisham* is fifty-six, so at this stage she must only have been about forty - but many years of living that way have apparently taken their toll.

[6] The drawing of curtains and stopping of clocks was a common Victorian signifier of death, and though these events predate the Victorian era, it's clear that Dickens meant to signify her feeling that she had died at a moment later revealed to be when jilted on her wedding day.

[7] Weak beer was still commonly drunk by children as well as adults in preference to water as the alcohol killed waterborne diseases - the first treated public water supply (in the world) was introduced in London in 1829, while the early part of the story is set in about 1812.

[8] A shilling was twelve pence in pre-decimal coinage, equivalent to a modern 5p, but worth a lot more in those days.

[9] Bank notes were not the colourful things they are now, but much larger sheets of white paper with the details printed in black on one side, so one might easily be mistaken for scrap paper by one unfamiliar with them as *Pip* and *Joe* would be. £2 was worth over £150 in modern equivalence.

[10] An indentured apprenticeship was a system going back to the Middle Ages whereby an apprentice's parents would pay a 'premium' to a craftsman who would then, over the next seven years or so, teach the youngster his trade. The system was breaking down by the time Great Expectations was set, and no longer compulsory for the old trades after 1814

[11] A guinea was originally a gold coin worth one pound, but, being made of gold, its value started to be higher than one pound. The value was fixed, for a while, at twenty-one shillings, but this officially ended in 1816. After that, although not an official unit of currency, it continued to colloquially to be used to mean one pound and one shilling - a usage that largely dies out with the introduction of decimal coinage in 1971. Today the term is only really used for prize money in horse racing circles. A blacksmith at the time might have earned £40-45 a year - possibly less in a small village such as *Joe*'s - so twenty-five guineas would have been worth a lot more than might be suggested by simply multiplying it buy a century's worth of inflation.

[12] As mentioned in note ix, this was no longer a legal requirement.

[13] A journeyman is technically a skilled artisan who has learned his trade but is not yet a master craftsman. The word *journeyman* comes from the French word *journée*, roughly meaning that which can be done in a day (from which we also get the more common journey, originally the distance that could be travelled in a day). A journeyman is thus a skilled labourer hired by the day - like a cover teacher or skilled agency worker.

[14] Schools often used to use slates, like mini-blackboards, for students to write on with chalk - the advantage being that they could be wiped clean and used tie and again. The presence of one such slate in the Gargery household has been mentioned earlier.

[15] According to Dickens' notes, *Miss Havisham* is 56 when *Pip* is 23, so she would have been about 51 at this stage, thus 26 at the time of the events described by *Herbert* which were seven years before *Pip*'s birth, and fourteen years before his first visit to *Satis House*.

[16] Dickens notes that he was three or four years younger than *Miss Havisham*, which, she already being passed the normal age for marrying, she might have found especially flattering.

[17] *Miss Havisham* would have been thirty-three or thirty-four at the time.

[18] Defined as 'an office or building in which the accounts and money of a person or company were kept', in this case, given *Herbert*'s interests, it would have probably dealt with shipping accounts.

[19] A baronet is a hereditary title, created in its modern form by King James I in 1611, which ranks higher than a knight but lower than a baron.

[20] It's not clear if *Wemmick* is aware of the significance of who *Jaggers*' housekeeper is - which is revealed in part three of the book. Ostensibly, he merely wants to illustrate *Jaggers*' power over people and Dickens uses it as a device to create interest in the character, but it could be that *Wemmick* is nudging *Pip* towards an important realisation.

[21] There is an actual Walworth Castle in county Durham which, though a much grander place, might just have sparked the idea in Dickens' mind.

[22] It's tempting to wonder if Dickens wasn't playing with the idea of *Jaggers* being in some way behind the future association between *Drummle* and *Estella*, but the idea is never developed.

[23] It is interesting, though perhaps not unusual, that *Pip* never learns this lesson: the only time that *Estella* has shown any interest in him is when he doesn't act in the wet way he does around her. This might have some bearing on her future relationship with Bentley Drummle.

[24] It should be noted that *Pip* has, by this stage, met both of *Estella*'s parents, but has no idea who they are. Maybe *Pip* is seeing something of one of them in her.

[25] And it shows the depth of *Pip*'s infatuation - and his hearing only what he wants to hear - that it can survive this unscathed, just it survives all *Estella*'s warnings to him

[26] It is never directly pointed out, but this, of course, makes her another *Miss Havisham*

[27] *Trabb*'s boy - knowing *Pip*'s humble origins, pretends to be in awe of this fine gentleman and pretends to be him dismissing the common folk with a 'Don't know ya!' in imitation of a posh accent. This of course does, in fact, reflect *Pip*'s actual behaviour to *Joe* back to him - but, as usual, *Pip* is blind to this and merely outraged.

[28] Admittedly he is probably still in turmoil, but *Pip* is throwing his weight around - getting *Orlick* sacked and withdrawing business from *Trabb* on account of his shop-boy in a way he doesn't back in London.

[29] The play is Shakespeare's Hamlet, and Claudius is Hamlet's uncle who murders Hamlets father to obtain the throne. *Wopsle*, of course, plays Hamlet.

[30] He knows this is absurd - she would have had to leave at two in the morning to be there by seven, and it is extremely unlikely any coach would even have been running at that hour - but he can't contain his nervous anticipation.

[31] *Pip* is in fact entirely free to follow his own devices, being in reality bound only by his love for *Estella*. *Miss Havisham* plays on *Pip*'s belief that she is responsible for his great expectations, but it is not clear whether *Estella* is playing the same game or genuinely believes that *Pip* is, like herself, one of *Miss Havisham*'s playthings.

[32] This, of course they cannot do because *Miss Havisham*, even if they convinced her, isn't responsible for *Pip*'s fortune.

[33] Like *Pip*, *Estella* would have represented a threat to the scheming relatives' plans to get their hands on all the Havisham fortune.

[34] Though still Georgian (c.1826) the arrangements seen typical of what we think of today as a Victorian funeral.

[35] High denomination bank-notes as high as £1000 - a huge amount of money in those days - were available from banks, but they were more like cheques in that they were made payable to a specific recipient and signed by hand. The notes were white, and printed on one side only. £500 notes were first issued between 1725 and 1745 and continued to be issued until 1943, ceasing to be legal tender in 1945. Like all high denomination notes, they were withdrawn because of increasingly sophisticated forgery.

[36] It is tempting to think that *Estella*, who knows she can't love *Pip* and frequently warns him of this, might have engineered this fight to help *Pip* understand the dynamics of the situation, but Dickens never in any way implies that this is the case so, if this is a valid reading, the scene would arise out of Dickens' intuitive understanding of his characters, not as a deliberate plot point for the reader.

[37] Gas street lights started to be introduced in London in 1807 using gas derived from coal. Expansion took off in 1812 and by 1828, the time that the story has now reached, the network would have been quite extensive. Gas lights didn't start to make it into the home until the 1840s, so domestic lighting would have been mostly by oil lamps with some candles still in use.

[38] This was theoretically the case, the penalty being in place until 1835, seven years later - but it seems that nobody was actually hanged for the offence after 1810, so Dickens might have been using a little artistic licence.

[39] This, and the sense that his status as the gentleman he always wanted to be depends on somebody so far from being a gentleman goes some way to explain Pip's somewhat heartless ingratitude. The terrible irony, of course, is that had he but known it, what tied him to Estella had in one sense been strengthened, not weakened, as we see in part 3.

⁴⁰ Dickens is deliberately a little ambiguous, having softened the ending under pressure from the original one in which *Estella* has remarried before he sees her again. The final published ending is a bit problematic in that there is no finality: though the fictional narrator would have known what happened next, he appears to choose not to tell us. If he had married *Estella* and was living happily ever after thus would be a remarkably frank autobiography, and why not let us know, but if he is still in the limbo of uncertainty at the time of writing, why hint at something different?

⁴¹ Reminiscent of the pride *Miss Havisham* shows in *Estella* - both *Estella* and *Pip* have been shaped by others to their own ends, even if both benefitted financially.

⁴² A common practice in law courts, with which *Magwitch* was very familiar.

⁴³ They seem to regard *Magwitch* as more animal than man - the idea that *Magwitch* might actually be hurt by having the dream that has long sustained him rejected out of hand doesn't at this stage occur to either.

⁴⁴ It's perhaps interesting that this didn't deter him from wanting *Pip* to be a gentleman - perhaps he was a better judge of *Pip*'s character than *Pip* sometimes gave him credit for.

⁴⁵ It appears that *Jaggers* had a sufficient reputation for *Magwitch* to sell his clothes to pay for him already, but he doesn't seem to have done *Magwitch* much good. Dickens, unusually, makes no attempt to explain this.

⁴⁶ Clearly fanciful, this is perhaps intended to suggest the extent to which *Pip* feels he is bonded to *Estella*.

⁴⁷ A very long walk, but one that Dickens had done on at least one occasion, so he knew it was possible.

⁴⁸ The term Dickens actually uses is 'Hackney chariot', a playful version of Hackney carriage - a term by which London taxis are still known today. At the time, of course, it would have been a horse-drawn vehicle. The term 'cab' is actually short for cabriolet - a lighter vehicle which was around in the early 19th century, but is not actually what *Pip* used -the word is used here for convenience.

⁴⁹ The phrase used is married 'over the broomstick' - a country custom that had no legal force but signalled something more than a casual relationship.

⁵⁰ Maybe £70,000 in today's money, though comparisons are difficult.

⁵¹ He uses this name deliberately to maintain the fiction that *Magwitch* and *Provis* are different people, to keep *Jaggers* officially ignorant of the fact, so that he can claim, if necessary, not to have known on oath. *Jaggers* is, of course, well aware that they are not. In fact Dickens (as *Pip* the narrator) uses the name *Provis* most of the time - these notes call him *Magwitch* simply because that is his real name.

⁵² It's very easy in our times to say 'of course they would want to know!', but even now there are some parents who for often complicated reasons, don't want to know the children they have given away for adoption, and we have to allow Dickens a greater knowledge than ours of the times he lived in.

⁵³ He is possibly being a little hard on himself, and it is perhaps worth noting that part of the good is not in the money itself - he could have cashed in his 'expectations' at any time but for his misgivings - but in the repair in relations between *Miss Havisham* and the one part of her family who were not after her money but needed it most.

⁵⁴ The place is identified in Chapter 55 as Cairo in Egypt. The Suez Canal had not been built at his stage, and Cairo was not under British control at the time, though it had been briefly before and would be again but Cairo was still a cosmopolitan city and an important hub for trade with the Middle East, Africa and India.

⁵⁵ Dickens seems to have had a time-scale in his head, but he doesn't always reference it directly in the text - it's reasonable to assume, though, that a number of weeks have passed since *Miss Havisham*'s accident.

⁵⁶ Although since 1794 passports were issued officially by the government, the obtaining of them was clearly much quicker. Photography, of course, didn't even exist at the time the novel was set and passport photos weren't used until long after, so the standards of identification would have been much lower.

⁵⁷ He seems very slow to recognise Orlick, who he's known since he was a small boy, but perhaps the circumstances mitigated against this.

⁵⁸ That is a person who has been transported to a penal colony and my not return to England.

⁵⁹ It is important to note that the obvious objection 'What about *Estella* -she's his daughter' , though not brought up, is in fact covered by Dickens when he describes *Magwitch* and Molly as having been married 'over the broomstick' - a country custom with no official status. They were not married in the eyes the law and any claim *Estella* might have, if it existed at all in law, would be very hard to substantiate. The fact that neither *Pip* nor *Jaggers* even raises this possibility suggests that this would have been understood, not just by them but by the readership at the time. Molly's claim would have been even weaker.

⁶⁰ It is an odd thing how ineffectual *Jaggers* is with regard to *Magwitch* at every stage of representing him. Whether Dickens had some purpose in this other than as a plot necessity is not clear, but the relationship is

complex: he disapproves of what *Magwitch* does in regard to *Pip*, and frequently makes *Pip* aware that he's only doing it because he's being paid to do it, but he nevertheless does it and takes the money.

[61] See note xxiv, part 2.

[62] To allow Magwitch to escape justice.

[63] As noted before, the passing of time, while probably clear in Dickens' head, is not 100% clear in the text. We know the attempted escape with *Magwitch* was in March, *Magwitch*'s trial was in April (the next month) and there are at least 10 days between *Magwitch*'s trial and his death. This gives a range of between two and six weeks for *Pip*'s illness, the implication strongly that it is closer to the latter.

[64] In a sense, of course, it is - but not in the way Pumblechook means it. If he had been better able to accept Magwitch's wishes for him - more grateful for his sacrifices - and been more grateful all those who had genuinely helped him, he would not have had a bad conscience about the money and could have come into his expectations before Magwitch's death.

[65] Miss Havisham asked *Pip* to write it - *Pip* asks *Joe* and *Biddy* to say it out loud!

[66] The novel as originally conceived had no chapter 59. The ending described in part 3 note I was part of chapter 58.

[67] He'd be in his mid-fifties by now, according to Dickens' notes. This last chapter is set about 27-28 years after the first

[68] As mentioned in part 3 note I, this wouldn't make much sense if the book had genuinely been written by *Pip* - unless perhaps he had been writing his story while in Cairo and hurriedly tacked a last chapter onto the end without waiting to see where events lead - but it makes a satisfactory romantic ending to the book as a novel.

Printed in Great Britain
by Amazon